ROSS HARPER & MURPH
SOLICITORS

BEYOND REASONABLE DOUBT

A Memoir

Ross Harper

BLACK & WHITE PUBLISHING

First published 2016
by Black & White Publishing Ltd
29 Ocean Drive, Edinburgh EH6 6JL

1 3 5 7 9 10 8 6 4 2   16 17 18 19

ISBN: 978 1 78530 065 3

A CIP catalogue record for this book is available from the British Library.

Typeset by Iolaire, Newtonmore
Printed and bound by ScandBook AB, Sweden

To Ursula

CONTENTS

ACKNOWLEDGEMENTS

My thanks to Maggie Wilson who overcame my Scottish accent and typed and typed numerous pages. She is a gem.

My thanks to my equally patient publishers and to Graham Lironi for his invaluable input.

Any proceeds from the book will be paid to the Ross Harper Foundation, which has so far given over £90,000 to help pupils at Hutchesons' Grammar School and students at the University of Glasgow and the University of Strathclyde. My thanks to Lorne Crerar and Basil Baird for looking after the charity.

INTRODUCTION

I am eighty years old, with a back of an eighty-year-old, the forgetfulness of a ninety-year-old, the mind of a forty-year-old and the spirit of a twenty year old. I live in Perth, Australia, having joined my daughter and son-in-law and four grand-children there in February 2011. My wife Ursula and I live next door to them in a fantastic climate. We have two other children – Robin and Michael – and three more grandchildren in Sydney. The journey from Perth to Sydney is as long as London to Moscow. The journey from Glasgow to Australia's Perth has been longer still, but it has been fascinating and the source of a lifetime of wonderful memories.

For the majority of my working life, I have worked as a lawyer. I established a law firm, which went on to achieve some success, have dealt with many interesting and high profile cases, have lectured in the principles of law and have acted as a political advisor for individuals and organisations. I have been active in politics throughout my adult life, standing in local and general elections for the Conservative Party in the 1970s.

My work has exposed me to a variety of difficult situations, in which my personal conduct has been brought into question, and I have been at the centre of damaging media attention. It has also introduced me to a wide variety of people in positions of great fame and political power, including the Queen, Nelson Mandela, Margaret Thatcher, Tony Blair and Omar Sharif.

I hope in this book to give an inkling of the kind of life I have lived and the cases with which I have been involved; to give an insight into the rich rewards to be had from a life in crime. And learning from business law that the main difference is that the clients dress better!

1

CHILDHOOD

In 1994 I attended a memorial service for Labour Party leader John Smith, who had been a great friend of mine, but had collapsed and died after a second heart attack. The service was held in Iona, his spiritual home.

I was driven by Lewis Moonie, a doctor of common sense with immense body weight and intellectual power, who had been a former Defence Secretary in the Labour government, until a fall out with Tony Blair. Seated next to Lewis was Gordon Brown, then Chancellor of the Exchequer. As we shared recollections, I said to Brown: 'Well, there is one thing that the Chancellor cannot tax... and that's memories.'

Quick as a flash he replied: 'I have someone in the Exchequer working on that.'

Fortunately, he failed and I live with memories – many, many memories.

I was born in Glasgow in 1935, so my earliest memories really begin in the late 1930s. The earliest itself is a curious one and it perhaps explains my life-long aversion towards gardening.

The British Empire Exhibition was held at Bellahouston Park in Glasgow in 1938 – an event which attracted twelve million visitors and included an international football competition – and my first recollection is my parents promising to take me. By the time the day arrived, however, I had caught a bad cold so the visit was cancelled and I was instead roped into helping my father do some weeding; a disappointment which would be enough to put anyone off gardening for life!

My father Thomas was a Church of Scotland minister – appointed in the Eastwood Parish Church in 1930 – so I was brought up in its wonderful old manse. This was the site of many of my earliest memories. It was a vast property with two acres of grounds. The Church of Scotland was obviously still doing well in those days.

In the grounds, we kept hens. To begin with, I remember they were kept in batteries – somewhat cruel – and then they were allowed free rein of the garden. One of the jobs to which I was assigned was to search for the spots where they laid their eggs. At one point, for some reason I cannot fathom in retrospect, a cockerel was added to our brood, and I recall that one particular hen managed to keep us from finding her laying spot. She emerged later proudly appearing with a following of chicks. I admired her stubbornness and cunning.

Being a son of a Church of Scotland minister, religion was always in the background of my childhood. I was a serious Christian once, but doubts have formed over the years. My son Robin and daughter Susan both attended Sunday school. At a fairly early age, Robin showed great scepticism and posed questions to me about Christianity and faith that I was unable to answer truthfully. Even now, I am not brave enough to say that I am a total non-believer. I call myself an agnostic, but find myself praying, with modifications, every night. The perennial wars and violence between religions and sects over the centuries are the main things that make me uncomfortable with religion.

My father, however, was a great man. He was modest, unassuming and fiendishly intelligent. He was born in late Victorian times in 1895. I only know this because he once left his passport on the kitchen table and I sneaked a look, an act which led to me getting a stern telling off. The times were very different then. There were much greater levels of distance between parents and children when I was growing up, and you would rarely get to know other people's ages. It was a great secret – almost as private as sex. My parents never mentioned sex or explained sexual intercourse either, nor did they willingly disclose their dates of birth to me, so I depended on my elder brother Murray for clarification on the facts of life.

My father was brought up in Ibrox. I know very little about his parents and was told almost nothing. I do know that his father worked in the shipyards and also did some work for the local council. In pride of place in our family home was a gold key that had been presented to my grandfather for the opening of a school. I seem to remember there were whisperings in the family that he may have come from Ireland, but I've never been able to confirm this. Other strands of my family tree, such as that of my mother's mother – the Simpsons – have been traced back to the early seventeenth century. Yet, my paternal tree only starts in 1895.

Father was the youngest of a large family. His oldest brother, James, was a noted ear, nose and throat surgeon. According to my father, his brother could look up people's noses and see a five-pound note! His sisters, Agnes and Elizabeth, were schoolteachers. Neither of them married or had children. My father had two other brothers, one of whom I believe moved to Australia and the other was killed in the First World War. Having graduated in Arts and Divinity from the University of Glasgow, Father briefly went to America to study Systematic Theology and was awarded the STM (Master of Systematic Theology), before going on to undertake his PhD in the same subject, which I once attempted to read but found to be impenetrable.

As a young minister, he was offered a modest position in a rural parish in Durisdeer in the south of Scotland. He settled in well, helped by a nearby farmer who allowed him to shoot on the land, which was very decent of him. I remember, much later, meeting the Duke of Buccleuch who, because of his shooting skills, vaguely remembered my father when he was minister in Durisdeer.

My father was indeed a sound shot. Where he picked up these skills I do not know, but I do remember seeing him in action on a farmer's land. There was an organised shoot on the opposite ridge, going after a rabbit in the gully below us. All the guns opposite missed and their dogs were in hot pursuit. I remember my father carefully aiming at the rabbit and me panicking that he would shoot one of the dogs instead by accident. However, he was successful and hit the rabbit cleanly with a single shot. Then one of the dogs picked up the dead rabbit and took it to the pukka people opposite. 'Well shot!' they echoed over the ravine but, by that time, I was incensed that our rabbit had been stolen. My father, understandably, would not, and did not, complain or ask for the return of the rabbit. A good lesson in diplomacy for me at an early age.

For most of his life, my father remained the minister of Eastwood Parish Church, an imposing building, and was given a healthy annual stipend for the time of £1,000, and provided with accommodation in the form of the nearby manse. Although this was a large building with its two acres of land, it was not without its issues, perhaps not uncommon ones for the time, and I still believe its dampness and dry rot contributed firstly to his ill-health and also then led to deafness after that.

After my father's death, on Christmas Day, 1959, at the relatively young age of sixty-four years, the family commissioned a stained glass window to be placed behind the family pew. I know that pew well, since every Sunday we sat in the family pew and, after the children's address, filed out for Sunday school. We only missed church four times a year, when communion was celebrated. As I grew older, I attended Boys' Brigade bible classes before the church, then attended the full church service followed by Sunday school. A lot of religion for one day, but that's how things were and what was expected of you, particularly as the minister's son.

My father, in the pulpit, was impressive; carefully spoken, articulate and reasoned. I started, despite my low attention span, to look forward to his sermons. The life of a minister is odd. Nothing much happens in the morning apart from the occasional funeral. He usually enjoyed a lie in with his breakfast being brought to him by my mother Margaret, a stockbroker's daughter whose father was a partner in Knox and Ross. During the week he set a day aside for parish visits, notice being given to the congregation on a Sunday, but the events which stand out in my memory are of Friday and Saturday evenings. On the Friday he would retire to his room and write a sermon in neat small handwriting. This would take several hours. On a Saturday evening he would retreat to memorise the sermon word for word; one could overhear his modulated lovable voice practising the sermon. I still have the sermons, and was later to use a few on occasion myself.

Our Eastwood Parish Church, which started off as quite wealthy, later fell on harder times and embarked on a saving programme. With by then no assistant minister, whose role included reading two lessons from the Bible (Old Testament and New Testament), my father asked me to come to the aid of the party. I was in my early twenties and, although nervous about my ability to find the particular chapter in the Bible pages, I jumped at the chance. I remember sitting on the platform next to the choir with a gown and, later, a hood, having taken great care to mark the Bible passage appropriately beforehand. Half the battle is being prepared, a valuable lesson I was to use later in life.

In our Latin class we learned 'Laborare est orare' – work is prayer. But the bug of public speaking in a church had begun to bite and I decided, for a variety of reasons, not least financial, to become a lay preacher. Armed with one of my father's sermons, which I'd memorised, I passed the test and proceeded to earn my way through university lay preaching at various churches in and around Glasgow, sticking in the main to a few tried and trusted sermons.

Later, as a married man living in Merrylee on the southside of Glasgow, I became an elder of the church, lay preaching long since forgotten. As an elder, one of my tasks was to deliver communion cards and I remember delivering one to a sheriff in Glasgow, though doorstop meetings were mercifully brief.

One of the fundamental principles of my life has been my dislike of intolerance, which stemmed from my younger days and no doubt from the morality I encountered throughout my younger life. I recall, for example, that Jews were not allowed into the Buchanan Bridge Club, where my mother played.

'Why on earth do we practise discrimination?' I asked her.

'Oh,' she replied, 'Jewish people are very noisy.'

This came as a lame, and most unsatisfactory reply.

I joined Hillpark Tennis Club, and discovered that Jews were forbidden there too. A young Jewish girl lived opposite, and it was with a heavy heart that I noticed her trudging with her tennis racket to a public tennis court. To my discredit, apart from wailing, I did nothing. But it weighed heavily on my conscience.

Catholics were also discriminated against. In Glasgow the larger law firms did not take on Catholics till the 1950s or 60s. 'It is not us,' explained one senior partner. 'It might upset the clients.'

What absolute piffle!

The Jewish people decided to open their own bridge club (and golf club) and when I joined I received a warm welcome. The proprietor was the renowned and world-famous player Albert Benjamin, who recalled that when he was taken by his family after early immigration to Glasgow he was walking the streets and was stopped by a group of youths interested in only one thing: 'Are you a Catholic or a Protestant?' they demanded to know.

Albert felt he was safe. He said: 'I am a Jew.'

'We don't care,' said the ringleader. 'Are you a Catholic Jew or a Protestant Jew?'

It was Jonathan Swift who said: 'We have just enough religion to make us hate but not enough to make us love one another.' And how right he was.

I remember, nearly seventy years ago, my father sermonising in a positive manner about the loss of childhood prayer:

'A child will pray every night and once we miss one prayer and then another and eventually the habit of childhood prayer is lost for ever.' I quoted this with approbation many years later when invited back to my old school, Hutchesons', to present the end-of-year prizes. As a self-confessed agnostic I pray every night, but I even change the Lord's Prayer.

I do not believe in intercessory prayers; praying for King and Country. My brother, when he was very young, prayed for everyone in the world apart from the Germans. My mother was not amused.

I was once asked to submit an article in the 60s by a fellow student, Donald Macdonald, who became a Church of Scotland minister. The article I wrote attacked the validity and efficiency of prayers for others; I know that there are many examples of those who see miracles, and it is tempting to believe that they exist, but I argued that, if one was to conduct a survey of all patients, could we produce a single medical opinion that praying from the outside helped in any way whatsoever? A resounding no.

In my opinion, and humble it is, a prayer ought to be privately one of thanksgivings for relatives, friends, health and a pledge to be better to others and more charitable. And, to revert to the Lord's Prayer, it has some sensible requests: 'give us our daily bread'; 'forgive us our debts as we forgive our debtors' (Scottish version) or 'forgive us our trespasses as we forgive those who trespass against us' (Anglicised) and 'lead us not into temptation'. But why on earth, for goodness sake, did we not preface these demands with a simple 'please'? I cannot resist changing the Lord's Prayer. We were taught 'Our Father which is in heaven'. I change that to 'who' and sometimes add the rider: 'if there is a heaven'.

The notion of spending eternity in heaven is mind-boggling. What on earth do we *do*? It reminds me of the story about the angler who wanted to go to heaven and catch fish after fish. When he died he found himself in a pleasant stream and cast his fly. He hooked and landed a fish. The next time he cast a fly he hooked and landed a fish, and the next and the next and the next and he could not put his fly in the water without landing a fish. It was only eventually he realised that he was not in heaven but in hell.

And as for hell, or the consigning to a fire for eternity, my father used to describe a man who went to hell and he was cold.

'Why on earth are you cold?' he was asked.

'I couldn't get near the fire for ministers,' he replied.

I am still a son of the manse. I miss the quiet and contemplation of the church. There is a Church of Scotland not far from me in Perth and, who knows, one day I might muster the courage to wander in. As Coleridge said:

> *He prayeth best who loveth best.*
> *All things both great and small.*
> *From the dear God who loveth us.*
> *He made and loveth all.*

2

SCHOOLDAYS

The Second World War started when I was four, and turned everybody's lives upside down. I remember asking my mother how long the First World War had lasted, and being convinced that the current war would be the same. I added four years to 1939 and was certain that it would be over by 1943. I was only out by two years!

Glasgow was one of the main targets for enemy bombers, because of the great shipyards on Clydeside. As children we learned the jingle:

> *Underneath the spreading chestnut tree,*
> *Hitler dropped a bomb on me,*
> *And if you want to see me*
> *Visit the Royal Infirmary.*

I still recall attending a pantomime in Glasgow with Will Fyfe and Harry Gordon, and hearing this song:

I am a barrage balloon blower-upper,
I blow up the barrage balloons.

My parents soon decided that evacuation was the only sensible option for me. Murray, my older brother, was already in attendance at Belmont House school in Newton Mearns, only seven miles southwest of the city centre and not really a safe distance from the shipyards, and I was due to start there later that year. Belmont House opened a boarding school at Moniave near Dumfries, nearly seventy miles south of Glasgow. Both Murray and I were duly dispatched. I have read accounts of evacuees being understandably terrified at being away from home and from their parents for the first time at such a young age. This was not my experience. I mostly remember being excited! At the age of five, I was the youngest child in attendance there.

The headmaster at Belmont House was a formidable man named Montague Dale. He had a terrifyingly prominent Adam's apple, and a penchant for using slipper and cane at the slightest excuse. He would later become a priest in the Anglican Church.

I spent my time drawing destroyers and Spitfires shooting down Messerschmitts, often in the large dormitory we had called 'The Hood'. The greatest impact the war had on us was the sinking of H.M.S. *Hood*. It was a dreadful moment in the war, one which momentarily shook the nation's confidence. But like all boys at that time, I believed we would win the war and I desperately wanted to be old enough to fight and do my bit. Alas, even with the war extending further than I had expected, it was not to be.

I remember enjoying the holidays and the mid-term visit from the parents when we would all crowd round the windows waiting for them to arrive. Five was perhaps a bit young to be separated from parents, but we were there because of Hitler and I admire the charity of my parents.

A couple of incidents at school stand out in my memory. The first was when my brother lost a large, unbelievably beautiful marble to another who was more skilled at playing than he was and had offered a deal he could not refuse. Silly bugger.

Another was when I was given a second cricket bat as a gift and one of the poorer students would have given his heart for it. My best friend also desired it greatly. What to do? I had no need for it and would have liked to have given it to my best friend, but my sympathy was with the poorer schoolboy, who would probably never have received a cricket bat for himself. My diplomatic skills, even at that tender age, took over and, at my suggestion, they both readily agreed to race for the bat. I knew well the poorer boy was the faster runner and would win and, sure enough, he did. Honour was satisfied all round and the bat went where it should.

So much for my diplomatic skills. What about my arrogance? By sheer good fortune I had the best conker at school. I could beat any other boy at the conkers game and I was so pleased and confident with my conker that I took it and banged it against a stone wall, thus proving its durability. I banged it twice and then three times, each time harder. Suddenly, the conker took revenge and split into a thousand pieces; a salutary lesson in pride and arrogance at a very tender age.

By the age of eight I had left boarding school, though I am not sure why. Either my parents had run out of money or perhaps they had thought by 1943 that the war was on its way out. Yet, I still remember that my father was an ARP (Air Raid Patrol) warden putting on his helmet, strapping on his gas mask and reporting for duty at a small kiosk. We all, of course, had gas masks.

One time German bombers had flown nearby and my father and his companion had had to duck behind a hedge. In fact, the bombers managed to hit Eastwood Cemetery and the rumour was that two bombs had landed on Hutchesons' playing fields at Auldhouse. Nevertheless, we happily played rugby there, ignoring the rumours. My brother and I had spent a year at Glasgow High School but, after threats of closure by the then Socialist council, my father decided to move us to Hutchesons' school, which was more assured of a future, founded by the Hutcheson Brothers in the seventeenth century.

At Hutchie we had classes of about forty pupils ranging in age from nine to twelve and, as the class was very mixed, I managed to pass the exams reasonably well. I remember having to declare whether one was a supporter of Queen's Park Football Club or Rangers. I'd never heard of either of them, having been away at boarding school, and chose Queen's Park as having the larger body of supporters – always being one for the silent majority. Queen's Park is an amateur team which was then in the first division, though eventually they got relegated and relegated again, but their home ground is Hampden, used for internationals. There was little seating in those days, apart from the stand and the terraces, and the ground held up to 131,000 people. There were so many that the crowd sometimes began to sway, which was well known as the Hampden Sway. And if Scotland scored, the Hampden Roar could be heard for many miles over the city. But I did not attend many football matches and, eventually, my father converted me to support Rangers, whose Ibrox stadium is in Govan, my father's home territory.

Going into senior school at the age of twelve plus was a different matter. A top stream of boys were put into classes

1A and 1B studying Latin and 1C and 1D studying French in their first year in senior school. Thereafter, the classes were split again. It was a matter of pride to be in the top sections, but I am not sure that it was necessarily the wise place to be. Certainly, Murray and I were in with the cleverest boys – that was undoubtedly a help and an example – but I suspect French and German would have been more useful in later life than Latin and Greek. I never studied hard at school, but sometimes enjoyed Latin and Greek as being somewhat different. I never learned French, although our classics teacher said that we could easily do so after school. I left school not really fit for the modern post-war European world – but I knew my *Iliad*.

Until I became a baker's salesman, during a university vacation, I never mastered the art of adding up quickly. There is a reason for that. When at school, we were given homework with a number of figures to add up. These were on a printed form and handed out to the whole class. I showed my early signs of curiosity and inquisitiveness and found that the answers were all printed in a book. I then used my pocket money to buy the book and spent time at the tennis court rather than adding up. This was to my discredit and, I suspect, did me positive harm when it came to maths. The only time I recovered was when I saw the baker adding up reams of complicated sums – the price of rolls, the price of cakes and so on – in his head and rarely getting it wrong.

In the early days in the junior school, we had all sorts and I soon learned how to fight – not a lot, but occasionally. Fortunately, my father was sufficiently prescient to take me to boxing lessons and, as a nine year old, I remember being the source of amusement as I turned up to the gym wearing tartan trews. But I was taught how to stand and to keep one arm forward – my left, being a natural southpaw. I didn't keep up the lessons for too long, but long enough for me to learn the rudiments and that was enough to take me through some of the toughies in the class – when they agreed to box, that is, rather than adopting other dubious methods of violence.

In senior school I achieved, amongst the masters, a better reputation. In the first term of each year I did not knuckle down, skimped where I could and enjoyed life out of school. These activities were reflected in the first-term exam results, which always gave me a severe shock and warning – knowing that I could be taken out of the top-stream class and put into another one. Well, I buckled down and, for the second term, was a different pupil with very different exam results.

One of my greatest friends was Douglas Alexander, who was another minister's son, from Eaglesham. Douglas was small but agile and, despite his height, acted as a superb goalkeeper. He was also always so cheerful and a great companion. I kept his companionship throughout university. The tragedy and triumph for Douglas, who became a minister himself, was between the two generations. The morning he was due to sit one of his Highers (the final exam in the fifth year) his father died and, when Douglas came into the exam – just in time – no one knew what to do or say. To my surprise, I was able to take him by the shoulders and mutter condolences. He passed his exam.

At the other end of the spectrum, Douglas's children reflected great credit to him. His daughter is Wendy Alexander, who was the senior Labour leader in Scotland and his son, Douglas Alexander, who had qualified as a lawyer and later found himself in Parliament, rising to the cabinet. Strangely enough, many years later, I was able to repay Douglas for all his kindnesses to me by lobbying hard and successfully that he be created a doctor of the University of Glasgow.

And then there was W.C. Gillespie. His parents perhaps had not noticed the significance of calling him William Chalmers because, needless to say, W.C. Gillespie became universally known as 'Flush'. He was an athlete par excellence, played in Junior Wimbledon, and was an exceptionally fine fellow. I haven't seen him for a year or two, but he was still playing tennis at the age of seventy.

But in every class there is a brainy one. We had Soapy Sutherland and his exploits were legendary. He was top in every exam and even when I came home with my own results my parents would ask about how Soapy had done. In the bursary exam, for which he sat a pre-university exam, he was top of the pile in Scotland. Soapy went on to study medicine and was actually believed to have failed one of his examinations. He practised as a successful and no doubt happy general practitioner. But, in my humble view, his prodigious talent was wasted.

During my senior school, perhaps out of boredom or perhaps because it's in my nature, I tended at times to be mischievous, for which I was punished occasionally. In those days, each master had a leather strap which was administered on the palms of the hands and caused some distress – especially on a cold day. There was a secret, which I learned, which was never misbehave if the weather is cold.

One of our masters, who supervised our cricket practice session and once criticised me for fumbling a ball, was always pacing up and down the room in mid-flow on some positively boring subject. At that time I had taken up fishing with a length of nylon. I recall attaching the nylon to a rubber and piercing a hole in the middle and, sitting in the front row, placing the rubber in the middle of the floor where the master walked. I was successful. He saw the rubber and, without breaking his flow of mind-numbingly boring rhetoric, bent down to pick up the rubber. I twitched it three feet away and still remember his face when he bent down, again and again the rubber disappeared! Fortunately, he took the jape in good spirits and I escaped without punishment. The rest of the class, needless to say, were delighted with my bravado.

We had an odd janitor called Mr Leech who used to order us all about whenever he could. On the last day of term we paid him back by informing the headmaster that the janitor wanted the desks out of the classroom and we all trooped out with the desks, leaving them in the playground. I never found out what happened after that but I imagine Mr Leech was not best pleased!

We had a master to whom I never took and, one day, in the spirit of impishness combined with bravado and mixed with stupidity, I made an excuse to leave the class and nipped, at a breathtaking sprint, to a nearby newsagent with a public phone. I then phoned the school and asked the secretary if I could speak to the master (in a disguised voice – as much as one can disguise a voice as a youngster). The message went down from the secretary and the master duly left the class to take the phone call. I banged down the phone and beat it back to the classroom as fast as I could, managing to arrive before he worked out that there was no one on the phone. What on earth made me do this I have no idea but I suppose it was good fun.

My closest brush with ill fortune came when I was in the sixth form and we were allowed to potter around the gym after school had finished. Douglas Alexander and I had a rugby ball and we were trying to drop the ball into the corners of an imaginary goal. Now I have never been a great rugby player, or indeed a competent kicker of the ball, but, for some reason, it was probably the end of the exams and I was in an exhilarating mood, I remember dropkicking the ball with considerable force.

Well I made the one deadly drop goal kick of my life and the ball soared thirty feet above Douglas's despairing goal-keeping hands and up and up towards a stained glass window depicting the Hutchesons' founders. Both our hearts were in our mouths. The punishment for breaking the window would have been horrific and the stained glass would have fallen into the street below and could have caused serious injury to a passer-by. The ball soared, onwards and upwards, towards the doom of the young Harper. I remember to this day that the ball hit the leaden strips in the centre of the window and did no damage. What a relief! We both scurried home, red-faced with embarrassment.

We played rugby and cricket at Hutchie. I started off claiming a knowledge of rugby and was put into the fly-half position, but, once others learned how to pass the ball and tackle, I was quickly sent into the scrum. I managed to emerge from the second row, which is bad for the ears, and became a wing forward, which is better for the ego. I never made, despite some efforts, the First XV, but was a regular of the Second XV and enjoyed the game. Scoring a try (which for me was extremely infrequent) is rather like fishing. The moments of scoring live with one forever.

I never made the Cricket XI at Hutchie. Tennis was different; I'd played tennis at home, had joined a tennis club and had become reasonably proficient. Unhappily, during the last year when I would have been certain to play for the school team, my appendix was removed and along with that flew out my chances of playing tennis that summer.

I recall my father saying that school days were the happiest days of your life. In frustration I used to think, 'If these are the happiest days then count me out.' But, in retrospect, they were most enjoyable, with companions, good friends and a large dose of reality. Along with Edith Piaf, I would have to say, 'I have no regrets.'

3

UNIVERSITY

At an early age my parents and relatives pestered me as to what I planned to do with my life. The answer 'I want to be a train driver' did not raise smiles of approval. The relevance of asking is, of course, that a choice may dictate a programme of study, not that there was much of a choice; Latin and ancient Greek were the order of the day.

Perhaps a Church of Scotland minister (my father's financially ill-rewarded occupation)? A definite no. Although, at one time I toyed with being a missionary, but not for long! A stockbroker? That was the job of my maternal grandfather. A positive no. My uncle had four children, all, like him, doctors. My brother had also decided to study medicine – and I sought peace and kept everyone happy by electing the same subject. I was given peace for a short time, that is, until my brother started working over the summer at a hospital. When he described how he had to wash dead bodies, I saw the light and, being squeamish at the sight of blood, changed my mind and said 'No way!'

That set the cat among the pigeons. What on earth was

I expecting to do? Study English? As a late developer and something of a shirker, my results were not sufficient enough to expect a First-class honours. How was I going to earn money?

I had read stories of great lawyers and barristers and, on analysing my capabilities, found debating and arguing at the top of the tree. I loved advancing propositions, however odd. My father took this seriously and introduced me to a parishioner who, as an advocate, was a part-time public prosecutor. He in turn introduced me to a trial in the High Court sitting from time to time in Glasgow. Yes, I was fascinated and determined to study law and become an advocate, without properly considering the severe financial barriers.

Family satisfied, I even paid attention in the Latin class and enrolled for a Master of Arts degree, which was an essential precursor to the LL.B (Bachelor of Laws). In those days one could alternate with a direct B.L., but I was confident of making use of my hobby of making money. And in these days, everyone received a grant of fees plus spending money.

At university, despite a then notoriously difficult Latin course run by an enigmatic, cruel Professor Christian Fordyce, I had a leisurely time – only occasionally attending classes, having realised that 51% was as good as 91% in an ordinary degree. I was therefore seduced into the Students' Representative Council, the Scottish Union of Students, and, the final accolade after the Presidency of both, Chairman of the International Student Conference. I had never been abroad in my life but suddenly found myself propelled to Ceylon (as it was then), Nigeria and Peru. But all that was in the future, when I was a law student.

When I was at school I was an active member of the debating society, which decided to hold a mock election. The popular party vacancies were soon full, but I decided that I would have to stand for the Communist Party.

This could have been a very unwise decision that could have affected subsequent entry into the United States at that time due to the McCarthy fears about Communists. Nevertheless, one of Murray's friends helped me with a humorous speech in which I promised that teachers would call us with the prefix 'mister'. I also promised a six-month summer holiday, a three-month Easter holiday and a three-month Christmas holiday. Needless to say I became very popular and came second in the election – second only to the Scottish National Party.

When I started at university we attended a Freshers' camp and were assailed by the speakers from the university representing all the parties. I listened to them all with scepticism. I remember the speaker from the Free Socialist Party because I frequently interrupted the debate. Most of my interruptions had been nonsensical but I was that sort of lad. I do recall cracking a joke at the expense of that particular speaker when I asked him 'Are you free?' After some hesitation he replied in the affirmative and I replied in a falsetto voice, 'That's nothing, you're free but I'm four!'

I was invited by the Conservative Club at the University to join and, after some hesitation, I did so. I liked debating and, unusually for a fresher, took part in the first debate at Glasgow University Union. These are grand affairs, lasting from lunchtime till two or three in the morning. I prepared a reasonable speech and won the maiden speaker's prize. This was quite an honour, although I had to wait till 2.30am to be presented with it.

I recall that, at the Latin class, I was approached by another young fresher, Jimmy Gordon, who congratulated me on my speech, and remarked that he thought I was a more experienced student. He was amazed that this had been my first debate. While I basked temporarily in his congratulations and wonderment, Jimmy Gordon went on to become a magnificent speaker himself, outclassing me, and is currently Lord Gordon, sitting splendidly in the House of Lords.

I quickly became convenor of the Forums of the Conservative Club, with responsibility for arranging guest speakers for the following year. This was an interesting task and I was able to write to Members of Parliament, inviting them to speak at the Union, a usually very well-attended Forum.

But my appetite for the Conservative Party was lost because I did not particularly like those in charge and because they insisted that, before one could speak for the Party, one attended a pre-debate night to discuss the issues. This was all very well for a normal student. Unfortunately, I was not a normal student and had so much activity connected with the Students' Representative Council and other issues that I simply could not find the time, nor indeed did I have the inclination, to attend these boring pre-debate discussions, so I soon fell out of favour with the Conservative Club. I like to think that this was not my loss.

My real interest in politics came when I decided to study both sides and purchased Penguin books on the case for Labour and the case for Conservatism by Quentin Hogg – who became Lord Hailsham – whom I met at a Law Society conference. Hogg's case for Conservatism was sufficient to convince me that if I was to retain an interest in politics then it would be for the Conservative Party.

My arts degree was leisurely. My finest ruse was in the first year. I had just been elected as a first year representative from the Arts faculty to the Students' Representative Council (SRC) where I wangled a place on the vacation employment committee. Why? The nose – get first in line for the job offers which flow in for the extraordinarily long vacations.

My immediate reward was to intercept a request for two students to act as river watchmen at the River Borgie in the North of Scotland. My father drove me there with the promise of a day's fishing.

Well our first day was pure misery. The river was unlet and we had to help the owner's gang net every pool and catch hundreds of salmon. And we knew that we were fishing there the next day. Some hope.

But they could not net the pool at the foot of the falls and there we repaired.

Tying two or three flies together we cast into the falls and pulled. And pulled. I sent a happy poaching father back in the car with a boot loaded with salmon. He was popular with his friends!

We helped dig peat in the morning and the rest of the day living alone in a bothy was ours. We were supposed to walk the river to scare off poachers and we did take the occasional stroll.

But we lived on salmon which I poached and our only shopping trips were to buy potatoes and mayonnaise. I am sure someone must have guessed. Salmon three times a day, for six weeks! Perish the thought.

And we were given a modest income. There was no sign of a flood and I must confess singular sympathy with the paying tenants the next week. A spate did eventually come and to my delight I caught a salmon properly on the fly. It went to the owner needless to say. Not too much of a worry though.

My task was not only to pass my degree exams with minimum attendance and as few resits as possible, but to acquire legal status as quickly as possible. Prior to my study it had been possible to complete the two degrees in five years.

The regulations had, a year or two before, changed this to a minimum of six for an ordinary first degree and seven for an honours. To hell with an honours; far too much real intensive work, thank you very much, and time was an enemy. I was also facing two years in the National Service.

Now I am, and always have been, hopeless at detail, but I pride myself on my ability to understand and manipulate regulation. I studied the six-year rule and found an adroit solution, although I was never totally confident in the outcome until after my second graduation.

To graduate I needed to pass seven separate and different subjects which, subject to constraints, provided a wide choice. I found out that if I passed six subjects in two years, I only needed one in my third. My next finding was that one of the arts subjects was Civil Law, which, subject to a slightly better performance, would qualify as one of the mandatory Law Faculty subjects. My real finding was that the final exam for Civil Law took place in March. I could therefore graduate some months ahead of anyone else. In the event, I did so. So far, so good. I had, of course, been advised to take another subject, and consented to be enrolled in elementary Italian. I managed one class and fled. But the real coup was to come.

I discovered that one law class, Public International Law, was to start after my arts graduation and so met with the law adviser for students (John Neill, a talented and engaging man in a city law firm who, happily, was also the lecturer) early in the term and established that the requirement of his course was to be enrolled in the faculty – and I was chasing an LL.B. to be an arts graduate.

Anyway, I was now in unchartered territory. But the argument, in my opinion at least, was sound and I was accepted. The next hurdle would be to convince the authorities that a Civil Law pass in arts, and a law pass in the late spring, constituted a year. I would never know until graduation enrolment two years later whether that argument would be accepted, and I was in dread of cancellation until the very last second, but accepted it was. It was good for the ego to break records.

Not that this triumph did me any good in qualifying sooner, since I had to complete a three year apprenticeship and consider National Service, but it was good to be a trailblazer and have a relaxed final year as an apprentice, mopping up on a few subjects dropped on the way, although not strictly necessary.

The apprenticeship came first and this shaped my whole life. The clerk to the SRC was a delightful lady, Mrs Ruby Whiteford, who, before joining the SRC, had been head typist in R. Maguire Cook & Co. She introduced and recommended me to them, and vice versa.

I was introduced to one of the founders, Cook, aged and aging – apparently a brilliant reparation king. His co-founder looked after criminal work and also had a good reputation, but had predeceased, leaving two sons, Kevin – reparation, and Francis – conveyancing and estates. Slash Martin was an ex-army, down-to-earth jack of all trades, although he would not pretend to be master of any. He was essential to the business as a motivator and organiser – earthy language – brandy and lunch with an illegal bookmaker followed by a large cigar in the office. Truly one of nature's wonders. We developed a terrific relationship.

But standing out in this most successful firm was Jim Murphy, whose court appearances displaying confidence, honesty, intelligence and stunning presentation, were a joy to behold. He helped me along with sage advice and had possibly the greatest effect on my life. And with him, after serving two years as a qualified assistant with Maguire, we founded Ross Harper & Murphy some fifty-five years ago.

And my two years' National Service? I was lucky. I had tennis elbow, which might have limited my ability to handle a rifle, so I applied for dispensation on medical grounds. I received a friendly inquisitor and was excused. I regretted this, but was extremely thankful.

I must confess I am not a particular fan of the Unions. When I was seventeen or eighteen I took a Christmas job as a temporary employee in the post office, working in George Square. The Christmas mail made sure everyone was busy. One of our jobs was to drag a sack containing mail to sorters. Noticing that they were eagerly awaiting more mail, I took it upon myself to drag two sacks at the one time across the floor. It was not too backbreaking and a genuine effort from a young student to help. But not so; I was stopped in my tracks by a man who identified himself, not as a foreman, nor as a supervisor, but as a Union official and I was roundly told off for doing too much work. Perish the thought.

When I worked as an apprentice at Maguire, we had to undertake investigations of accidents in factories – mostly for the pursuer and occasionally for the defender (an insurance company). I still recall that a workman for whom we were acting had suffered dermatitis and the management was at pains to point out that workers were instructed to go into the toilet where a certain form of cleansing soap was provided. When we went into the toilet, I noticed a number of men sitting on the floor with their backs against the door, smoking nonchalantly. When we left, as an eager and inquisitive youth, I asked the chap who was showing us around whether these workmen were on their break. He replied that they were not.

I then expressed some amazement that management did

not take steps to remedy the situation and was told that the management was forbidden from entering the toilets and no steps could ever be taken. The power of the Unions. How I mourned for British industry.

In October 1956, the Hungarian revolution took place. It was immediately stamped out and there were many refugees fleeing by crossing the Danube into Austria. A number of the refugees were, unsurprisingly, students. Well, students respond to students, and a meeting in Vienna was called. Douglas Alexander was President of the Students' Representative Council and I was President of the Scottish Union of Students at that time. We approached the Principal of Glasgow University, Sir Hector Hetherington, and explained that we must attend the meeting of students in Vienna. Immediately, he summoned a cheque and we were on out way.

While there, we visited the borders and watched with amazement as refugees swam over the Danube, one of whom had a bullet hole in his wellies! On returning from Vienna, we set up the Hungarian Students Rehabilitation Appeal with enormously successful results and welcomed Hungarian student escapees to universities in Scotland. One of them went on to become Professor of Law at Strathclyde University.

As a student I had vacation employment with the *News of the World*, one of Rupert Murdoch's salacious newspapers, which no longer exists. My job was to meet the train from London at six o'clock on a Sunday morning and fill a van full of copies of the paper. We then proceeded to distribute them around a fairly large area. During the week, my job was to visit all the newsagents that had taken supplies of *News of the World* and collect the money.

The good news, as far as I was concerned, was that I could

keep the van all the time I was doing this, although my father and his friends must have raised more than a few eyebrows when the *News of the World* van, emblazoned with the paper's logo, was parked outside the manse. It didn't stop me being able to run girlfriends from the tennis club dance to their home – and indeed was much coveted.

One of my most fortunate coups was when I was about to graduate as a lawyer. I knew that lawyers were employed by the daily papers in Scotland to check each night for libel (in Scotland called defamation). As I was an apprentice, I frequented the Glasgow Sheriff Court and discovered that the lawyer (Bill Dunlop, since deceased) who 'legalled' for the *Express* on a Tuesday was about to leave. Now John Neill, the man in charge, a senior lawyer in Glasgow, was the lecturer in public international law and adviser of studies who had helped me graduate in two years rather than three, due to my delicate circumvention of the rules. So I decided, barefaced, to approach him and said that I would dearly like a job of an evening in the *Express*.

He was a charming, polite man who sympathised with me immensely and was able to say that he would love to have me, but that the slots were all full. And here was my stroke of genius – I was able to inform him, before he knew, that the Tuesday night slot was about to become vacant and poor John Neill, I suspect, was hoisted with his own petard of decency. What could the poor man do but offer me the job? As it happened, although I graduated, I still wasn't fully qualified, since I had to complete a three-year apprenticeship, but I was the last to tell him that!

In any event, I worked every Tuesday from seven o'clock till one o'clock for the princely sum of four pounds a night and, as others grew older or lazier, I was able to act as a travelling reserve, filling in and sometimes doing two or three nights a week. My pièce de résistance was to keep the editor – with the greatest of difficulty – out of jail.

A late story had come in that a well-known footballer had been arrested in Aberdeen and was being charged with some offence, such as indecency. The story was short, but a photograph of the footballer appeared in the proof sheets. I explained to the editor that, where a person was accused, under the law of Scotland no photographs could be printed of an accused in a newspaper. The editor (Roger Wood – an enormously energetic and bullying man who had come up from England) snorted in derision. He then turned for advice to an experienced assistant editor, whose job was to sit beside me and proofread as well, who also snorted and said that the footballer was well known and that everyone knew his photograph. If Churchill, he reasoned, was charged with an offence, surely the papers could print a photograph of Churchill?

I was discomforted and worried and phoned John Neill at his house for advice. He confirmed that, under no circumstances, should or could the photograph be printed. Thus emboldened, I approached the editor directly again (this was unusual since most of the dialogue takes place with assistants or sub-editors). He continued to snort and said that he would print the photograph. I was, in terms of experience, knee high to the giants of the land, but I was comforted inasmuch as I knew I was in the right. I looked him in the eye and said: 'You have my advice. This advice is supported by John Neill. If you print this I shall visit you in prison!'

I could see realisation dawn on his angry face and he suddenly called out 'Stop the press!' – since the papers were just starting to print – and the offending photograph was duly removed. Needless to say, I was not thanked for holding up production.

A fortnight later, when I was on duty, a copy of the *Evening Times* lay on my desk and the headline there read '*Record* (another Scottish newspaper) was fined £5,000 for contempt of court.' With the sub-heading, 'If the editor had been on duty, he would have gone to jail.' Trying to hide my glee, I showed this to the assistant editor sitting beside me, who read it and I still remember that he was unwilling to admit fault in any way and dismissed the High Court ruling with the remark, 'They were wrong.'

Around this time, as I was starting to establish myself, my father died. He had been very ill for some time and his bed was moved to the lounge. He suffered from chronic bronchitis and his lungs seemed badly affected and he weakened visibly. Eventually he was taken into hospital and, on Christmas Day 1959, I went in to visit him in the early afternoon.

My mother was due to come in some two or three hours later and, thereafter, with Murray and his wife Charlotte, we were going to repair to a restaurant for Christmas dinner. It required to be early because I was due to serve as a duty lawyer in the offices of the *Express* on Christmas night – not a greatly sought after date by the other lawyers. But I was the junior one and, like Barkis in *David Copperfield*, was always willin'.

When I arrived at the hospital, the specialist asked me when my mother was due and I replied that it would be two or three hours later. When he pulled a face and muttered 'Too late,' I sensed that something was dreadfully wrong.

I approached my father's room with trepidation. He was barely conscious but watching a circus on television – of all things! I remember he grasped my hand and went off to sleep. I arose and paced the room wondering what to do when, suddenly, his breathing became more laboured and finally stopped.

I rang such bells as I could find and a nurse came in and held his pulse. I still remember choking, 'Is he... is he... is he dead?' The nurse felt his pulse and put the bedsheet over his head, nodding mournfully.

This was Christmas afternoon and tragedy had struck the Harper family. I telephoned my brother, who immediately went round to my mother's house to break the news. I gave him time and then went home. But what can one say to a grieving wife – especially when one is a grieving son? My brother was shrewd enough and warned me when I entered the house to say that my father had never been conscious when I entered the hospital. If she had known that I had spent his last minutes alive with him, she would have been mortified and self-critical that she had not come with me.

Arrangements were made for Murray to take my mother to his house. Time was passing, I had to shake myself out of my stupor to attend to my duties at the *Express*. I managed to get into the *Express* and went to my usual seat. I was late, but not desperately so. I waited for some shouts of 'Merry Christmas', but none were forthcoming. The room where I worked was full of editors at the top desk with many sub-editors feverishly working away, polishing up news copy.

As I took my customary seat, Roger Wood, the editor, shouted at me, in the hearing of everyone, that I was late and started to verbally abuse me. It is unheard of for a lawyer to be so abused – especially in front of such an audience. I said nothing and merely sat down, whispering to the assistant editor beside me, a senior man, that my father had died an hour or so ago.

Quick as a flash, the assistant editor strode up to the editor and whispered my news in his ear. Within seconds, the editor rushed over to me profusely apologising and indeed asking if I wanted to go home. Nevertheless, I was on duty, and duty comes first, even though it was Christmas and even though one had lost one's father an hour or two earlier. Word quickly swept through the room and I was treated with care, kindness and condolences, all of which helped repair some of the damage in my heart.

In the *Express* we worked late, usually till about one in the morning, and when I got home I staggered into bed to be woken the next morning by the doorbell. One of the ministers in charge of Glasgow Presbytery had heard the news and came to pay his condolences. I greeted him as a sorry sight in my pyjamas. My mother had gone to my brother's home.

There was a funeral service held in the church, which was packed, and only a few were invited to the graveside. My father is buried in Eastwood Cemetery. Someone had purchased a certificate for four people to be buried in a plot there and a suitable tombstone was later erected. I have only visited the grave on two or three occasions, one of which was particularly sad because my brother's ashes were scattered over the family grave in the seventies.

My mother remarried and, when she died, was cremated with her ashes scattered at the crematorium in the same place as the ashes of her second husband. But in the autumn of life we are in death. I keep changing my mind about what should happen to me when I die, not that it is anything to do with me and nor should I care. My first thoughts were that I should be cremated and my ashes consigned to the River Tay, where I spent so much time, fun and enjoyment fishing for salmon. Now I am not so sure. Why impose on anyone else? A quick cremation. Don't bother about the ashes. A fond farewell. Worry no one, nor inflict anything on their memories.

I did not last more than three or four years at the *Express*; the pay was miserable and the hours long, but it was, at the time, most enjoyable. I have since contributed to many papers. My main triumph with the press was to note that they paid for stories that were good enough to print. And Glasgow University was full of stories. Along with another fellow member of the university magazine, George Thaw, I set up the HT News Agency. HT stood for Harper Thaw. Donald Dewar, who was to become First Minister of Scotland, but was then a gawky student, became one of our contributors.

Eager as ever to make money, I toured all the newspaper offices in Glasgow – there were four or five of them at the time – and secured accreditation for HT News Agency so that the stories would be accepted and cheques made payable to the agency. It was not a runaway success, but a comparative one, and contributed to our income.

At about that time I had just started my apprenticeship with Maguire Cook and I printed a card, but I foolishly put the telephone number of Maguire Cook along with my home telephone number so that newspapers could contact me.

To my misfortune, one of the partners found a card and noticed the office telephone number was on it. It would be no exaggeration to say that all hell broke loose. I thought I may be fired. The least I expected was to be ordered to reprint the card. As it happened, one of the partners took me aside and instructed me to take every card and score out the office phone number. Somewhat relieved, I gladly acceded to his request.

After I was qualified, and I served as President of the Glasgow Bar Association, I was approached by *The Scotsman* to write an article that day on some legal matter – on which I must have given some off-the-cuff comment. I was busy at court but accepted the challenge and, in my usual delegating way, phoned somebody whom I knew in the Law Society to ask them to do a draft. Unfortunately, I couldn't get through to anyone and was left with no one to help. I was stuck. I knew a little about the subject, but not a lot. But for an intelligent newspaper article sometimes a little is more than enough, and I dictated fairly quickly what I thought was a reasonable article with plenty of argument.

In any event, it was despatched and duly printed and I was delightfully surprised when I was approached by *The Scotsman* and asked if I would like to do a weekly article on current law issues in Scotland. Delighted was an understatement and I buckled to this request – although I missed the first week because I got the dates wrong and had thought I was due to start the following week.

An assistant editor was placed in charge of me and he was a delightful, understanding man. I had an abundance of ideas, plenty of thoughts and, on a Sunday evening, would draft an article for typing and despatch the following day. But all good things come to a halt and I soon ran out of brilliant ideas. I remember on a Sunday sometimes asking myself 'What in the hell am I going to write about?' Usually, in the course of the week before, I had picked up some germ of a thought. I'd even written about Barney Noon, a long-time client and part-time plunderer. It was Sheriff Irvine Smith who composed the refrain about Barney: 'Thirty days hath September, April, June and Barney Noon.'

Often, when I was stuck, I would look at the latest offering of the Scottish Law Commission and always commended them for their work and diligence. My articles were obviously popular with them and used to be pasted on their noticeboard.

BBC Scotland was also a good provider of income. I was somehow adopted on to a radio programme in the sixties to discuss various issues in the morning and once a month my dulcet tones on the issue of the day could be heard speaking with authority on a subject about which I suspect I knew little. But my big breakthrough came with STV in the sixties. There was a programme called *What's Your Problem?* and it always had a five-minute legal spot. I was privileged to be part of that spot for some years; at first it is awe-inspiring and then becomes second nature. Again, I learned that a little knowledge is enough. Those who know too much about a subject can be devastatingly boring and, indeed, hesitant on a TV programme. The producers were looking for something short, snappy and lively. The poet once said, 'A little knowledge is a dangerous thing.' I would say in response to that, when appearing on radio or television, too much knowledge is considerably more dangerous!

4

EARLY YEARS

When I started the practice of law there was no such thing as criminal legal aid. If a probable cause was stated in a civil action, then legal aid could be granted, but criminal solicitors were not the salt of the earth. There was, however, in the 1960s and earlier, a system of criminal representation for the deprived called the 'Poor's Roll'. Solicitors were automatically put on the Poor's Roll and their duty was to appear for one week, sometimes two weeks, a year interviewing those in custody in the cells and appearing for them in the court. I think the sum of £30 was paid for the week's work. But this roll was good for the younger solicitor, since he or she, by that means, was introduced to those charged with crime and he or she could, if they were able, build up a respectable criminal practice. The governors were Willie Glen and later J.P. Murphy.

The court met at 2pm each day and the duty solicitor appeared in the cells some two or three hours before then to interview those who had been charged and kept overnight. There were either two or three solicitors on duty each time.

When the police brought the clients in to an interview room one at a time, they would sometimes whisper how much money (if any) they had in their possession when arrested.

The money in their possession was relevant to the amount of bail offered since bail money at that time was asked for in most cases. The secret was to get the money from the client and pay the bail directly to the Office of the Sheriff Court, and have the bail bond put in one's own name – which acted as a security for the fee (as long as the accused turned up and bail was not forfeited when the fee disappeared with the client).

In these days life was fraught with monetary danger. I remember appearing for someone pleading not guilty and a trial was fixed. There were seven charges of cheque fraud. Despite numerous reminders, the client never appeared at the office and I was left with nothing and a hopeless file. Suddenly, in the late afternoon before the trial, the client appeared. I told him that I would not appear for him unless I received a fee. The handling of trials was not part of the Poor's Roll system.

The man quickly and adroitly said he would pay and produced a cheque. I was wise enough to comment that I would not take a cheque since I did not wish to be a witness in a probable eighth charge! The scene we had in these days was NFNP – which stood for No Fee No Plea. Payment for a criminal solicitor was always subject to the gravest of abuse but, on the other hand, many willingly paid. As far as I recall, no cash was forthcoming, so he was on his own!

When we had just started, and I was relatively raw, I appeared for a woman charged with reset (receiving stolen goods). She lived with a man who had brought stolen goods into the house and had already pled guilty to theft. Since the value of the goods was high, she was charged before a sheriff and jury and could have been liable to a year or two in prison

– very different from a summary case which has a maximum of six months in jail, but more often a fine.

She had a bail bond of £30, which she agreed would represent my fee. Although this case must have taken place more than fifty years ago, I remember it clearly. On the surface she had little chance, but I had an inspiration. In Scotland there was at that time such a thing as common law marriage, meaning that a person could be held married by 'habit and repute'. Two persons living together and appearing as man and wife can, under the law, be presumed to be married. In the course of the jury trial, I tried to establish that the two were married by habit and repute. The second part of my argument was that a wife cannot be guilty of reset of the goods stolen by the husband. That makes total sense, and at that time it was the law.

In a dramatic moment, the jury accepted both arguments and my client was acquitted. After receiving congratulations all round, and no doubt basking in them, I turned to collect the bail bond from my free client. But she had disappeared. I repaired quickly to the Sheriff Court main office (about ten minutes away) and went to the bail office to intercept. I was too late. She was fleeter of foot than I was. The bail bond had been uplifted and I never heard from her again. I became a sadder, but wiser man.

Appearing for no fee was no isolated event, although not one for which I ever planned – except the odd case in which we had sympathy for the client. I used to have up to fifty files along the floor of my room. When a new assistant arrived, I would begin his education as I pointed to them explaining, 'See that mountain of work – no fees were ever paid.' NFNP – no fee no plea.

In my early years in law after my apprenticeship with Maguire Cook I took on a post at McGettigans, a pleasant two-partnership (brothers) firm at 65 Bath St. Restless as ever, I started a firm called Student Enterprises around 1960. I took in as a partner an electric former fellow student, Kenneth Fee. A virtual whirlwind of energy and redolent with ability.

We set up offices in 65 Bath St next to my office in McGettigans and secured easily the advertising contract for the students' charity magazine *Ygorra*. No great profits there but we found out that the firm who had previously been appointed produced newspapers on charity day throughout the city, carrying a mountain of local advertising and making a mint of money. What a gold mine, and they operated throughout the UK.

A lesson learned and information exploited. Luck of course helped. The firm doing nationwide business was called MacMillan Graham, owned by a large chap with a larger car. He would tour the UK roping in students and produce in Manchester from top to toe their annual charity magazines. And, of course, the hidden newspapers, disclosing perhaps one out of a dozen or more.

And out of luck, we were approached by a couple of former employees of MacMillans who were professional salesmen – youthful enough to wear a university scarf and sell the universe.

Using our university contacts throughout the UK, we, like Topsy, grew and grew. To cut a very long story short, we proudly took over (bought out) MacMillan Graham, taking over a splendid office and staff, then, of course, Lancaster Partners (our professional selling team) kicked the traces and offered to buy us out.

I regretfully fell out with Fee. We were both offered that same amount for our shares. I accepted but he thought we would eventually get more, but minority shares are, as I have often learned, worth sod all.

Legal Aid was finally, after much protest and lobbying, introduced for criminal cases in the early 1960s. Legal Aid means that the government, through a legal aid fund, pays out 'reasonable' fees. I was lucky enough to be in practice through its halcyon days. Appropriate fees were now paid for those appearing for the first time in custody. If an accused was charged before a sheriff and jury, legal aid was granted at a very early stage in the proceedings. In summary cases, where the maximum prison sentence was six months, legal aid was granted if there was a stateable defence.

One time, when I was sitting as a part-time sheriff at Dumbarton Sheriff Court, the solicitor Brian Adair appeared. I knew him well through the Law Society and he later succeeded me as President. When he saw that I was sitting in Chambers, he became cheerful and nonchalantly pushed a legal aid application for a petition case before me. I still remember his face when I said 'Legal Aid refused'. Now this refusal was not open to me, but I was playing him a jape. I eventually turned to the Sheriff clerk and asked, 'Do I have to grant this automatically?', and then I granted it.

After some years, despite much protest, a limit was put on the amount paid in a sheriff and jury case unless the sheriff or judge certified it as a case of unusual length, difficulty or complexity (a Section 13[2]). I once had a sheriff in Paisley, Sheriff Inglis, who was also one of my bridge partners – or to be more accurate, I was one of his – as a guest for fishing and sent him home with a large salmon, which delighted him. As he held it up and admired it, he said, 'This is worth a Section 13.2'.

Little did I know, but when I appeared at a sheriff and jury case, having employed counsel, he asked Sheriff Inglis at the end of a lengthy case to ask for a Section 13.2 certificate. The sheriff waved his hand and, before counsel could properly enunciate his request, the sheriff said 'Granted'. Needless to say, I was very pleased.

My certificate did not come through the post as it normally would have and, when I made enquiries of the sheriff clerk, I was told that it was not granted and the sheriff thought he was certifying the appearance of counsel, a certification which was not necessary in these days. This prompted much angst and the passing of numerous messages to and fro but, finally, my Section 13.2 certificate did arrive.

In my day there were two very famous criminal lawyers. The first, in the autumn of his life, was Laurence Dowdall, who was nothing short of electric, although, since he was near retirement when I started to qualify, I did not hear him in his prime. He made one mistake, however, by being too effective! He was appearing for Lionel Daiches, a former QC who was sitting as a sheriff at Glasgow Sheriff Court. Unhappily, Daiches was no stranger to drink.

In fact, the story goes that, at one time he was walking along the street outside the Court of Session in Edinburgh, swaying slightly. A judge stopped him and said reproachfully – 'Drunk again, Daiches.' Daiches, it is alleged, quick as a flash looking reproachfully at the judge and said, 'I am sorry to hear you are, my Lord.'

In any event, the police eventually caught up with Daiches one evening and he was charged with driving while under the influence of drink, a most unusual charge for a sitting sheriff. The case was taken at Glasgow Sheriff Court and a sheriff from outside Glasgow was called in. Dowdall delivered a masterful plea, which was printed over a page of the *Evening Times*, stating that his client, Daiches, had taken some pills and was inadvertently over the limit. He then described how Daiches had fought bravely during the war. He gave a heart-rending plea that Daiches should keep his licence. Contrary to normal practice (in fact 99.99% of 'drunken' drivers lose their licence), the sheriff was so moved by Dowdall's plea that he fined Daiches, but did not impose the normal disqualification. The story goes that, needless to say, Daiches was over the moon and repaired to his room to phone a former colleague now sitting as a judge – Manuel Kissen – to inform him of his good news. As Daiches chortled over the phone, Kissen knew better and said that this was not good news for Daiches.

And Kissen was absolutely right; it certainly was not good news. Why should a sheriff be treated differently from all the rest of the mortals? Would this not set the most unhappy of precedents? The storm grew, the newspapers were scathing and Daiches eventually lost his job as a sheriff, whereas he might well have kept it had Dowdall simply muttered apologies. The licence would be forfeited and the case would not have made headlines.

Succeeding Dowdall as the most prominent Glasgow criminal lawyer was Joseph Beltrami. He was serious, long-winded and at times pompous with a wide clientele and a flair, combined with an energy and capacity for publicity. I learned a lot from him about the importance of publicity in the criminal profession and was adept to follow in his footsteps, albeit in a slightly different way.

He eventually brought in a partner, a most likeable chap called Willie Dunn. He was a former prosecutor at the District Court and was competent, but without Beltrami's long windedness. Beltrami was so famous that people wanted him to appear for them. In fact, the saying goes that when Willie turned up for a trial, the client was heard to observe, 'Ask for Beltrami and get Dunn!'

Willie Dunn and I had a good relationship and we arranged to swap 'doublers'. This means that if one was nominated by two accused on the same charge sheet it was normally prudent, and on many occasions essential, to separate and arrange for a separate lawyer to represent one of them. We normally had the power when separating to nominate, or at least recommend to the departing accused, the name of another solicitor and Willie and I swapped doublers to good effect.

I recall that we repaired every three months to an excellent restaurant, and a luncheon with Willie meant that one had to write off the afternoon. Once I had had more than enough wine, as he had, out would come the orders for the brandy. I could not keep up. I suspect very few people could.

An interesting story was told about Beltrami. He used to dine in a very good restaurant in Bothwell where he lived and, of a Sunday evening, he would invite the local priest for dinner. While they were having dinner with plentiful wine, his son noticed that the label of the wine bottle was peeling off and that there was a different label underneath. Eventually, he managed to obtain his father's attention and Beltrami seized the bottle and, seeing the different inferior label underneath, called over loudly for the waiter. When the waiter appeared, he tried to take the bottle from Beltrami who said, 'You're not getting the bottle. This is evidence!' The waiter tried to wrestle 'the bottle from Beltrami, who then took the offending item and ran out of the restaurant, pursued in vain by the waiter. Whether the story is apocryphal or not I do not know, but Willie Dunn very much enjoyed telling it.

I rarely touched alcohol. Why? I was lucky – at a tennis club dance I spotted one of my tennis heroes absolutely gutted, reeking of alcohol and sick as a parrot. Not for me I thought.

This was a busy time in my life. I would do legal time at the

Express two or sometimes three times a week, lecture or rather talk on simple legal issues to patients at Philipshill hospital (collected rather dramatically by an ambulance), lecture to rotary clubs in Airdrie and Coatbridge, spent Saturday afternoons reporting (briefly) on rugby matches for the *Sunday Mail* and Edinburgh's *Evening News*, and preach on occasional Sundays. Quite.

5

EXPANSION

Despite all my political and extracurricular activities, Ross
Harper & Murphy flourished. Having started the office
on the first floor of Holland Street in the early sixties,
we were successful and bold enough to move to larger
offices in West George Street and started to employ more
staff. And Glasgow drama unfolded. A severe storm and
damage to a number of buildings. Three or four floors up
from us a large chimney stack succumbed to the gale and
crashed effortlessly through all the floors ending up on my
desk in the basement. When we tried to enter the next
morning we were stopped by a stout Glasgow bobby... no
admittance!

But we had several court cases that day and no idea even of
the names. What to do? Cunning and resource was required.
I diverted the policeman to the side of the building with a
'query', Jim Murphy nipped in and retrieved the diary and we
escaped to the court where our pleas for continuation were
understandingly received. One punter who wanted his trial to

proceed was given short shrift. The exciting life of a Glasgow solicitor.

We then moved to even larger offices in St Vincent Street. They were for sale by the Church of Scotland and, after a survey, I managed (with some difficulty I may say) to persuade my partners that we should buy the whole building. That was confidence about the future!

We put in a moderate offer two days before Easter, allowing for a forty-eight-hour acceptance. I still remember being told that it was wrong to put the Church of Scotland under pressure over Easter, but commercial considerations in my mind outweighed anything else. The deal was done and the move to St Vincent Street was a great success, although we had acres of unused space. Eventually, however, it became too small!

We even had an opening office party, inviting amongst others the President of the Law Society (the late Jimmy Sutherland) to add some real gravitas to the move. Jim Murphy, in his inimitable fashion, wrote the invitations by way of a lengthy poem.

At that time we were expanding into other areas. Why on earth, when we were already running a successful practice, should we contemplate expansion upon expansion? Looking back on it, I think one of the principal motives in my mind was, strangely enough, to avoid tax. At that time, in the late sixties and early seventies, tax rates were very high and if one earned a lot of money one could end up paying 80% tax. Surely it would be better to reduce our profit by spending money opening up other offices? The other reason was that, in my untutored mind, we should fill an unmet need.

The practice of law was understandably, and I suspect correctly, criticised by other bodies as being unhelpful for the ordinary man and woman in the street. Most offices didn't open on a Saturday morning (we always did) and most offices shut their doors at 5pm in the evening. And a bus fare from some of the outlying areas into Glasgow would strain the humble purse, making the prospect of visiting our law firm even less appealing for many.

The answer in my mind was to open an office in these outlying areas, and so we did, in Castlemilk and Easterhouse, always taking a shop front. Needless to say, there were unbelievable planning pressures against a shop being used as a solicitor's office, but I invoked the help of many of my political colleagues and, eventually, we managed to open our shops in those areas.

There was plenty of business, but the success of these offices depended on the ability of the partner responsible to make that relative success profitable and, as importantly, liquid. Any excuse to open an office was seized upon. John Cross, a lawyer based in Airdrie, wanted to retire and we purchased his office. The office of Cruikshank of Hamilton became available and we took it on. Ronald McMath of Rutherglen died and we took his office too.

We opened at Kilmarnock, Ayr, Tollcross, Kirkintilloch and at one stage we had twenty-three offices. Perhaps, in retrospect, we expanded too fast. Not all partners were up to standard and a successful office required first class partners and first class assistance. In fact, two of our partners, after they left under somewhat difficult circumstances, landed up in jail.

My greatest regret was the young McCluskey. He was a young apprentice and then a solicitor with us and I must confess I was taken with him and treated him like a son. He was a fantastic worker and lived in Kilmarnock. I remember at the beginning, when we bought him a car, (before that I lent him one) he would come to the house to give a lift to myself and the children (to school) or we both repaired to the office.

As he lived in Kilmarnock, what better to do than to open an office there? There was considerable local opposition, and I recall visiting a number of Kilmarnock offices in an effort to assure them that we would be concentrating on criminal work and would not be interfering with their comfortable conveyancing or commercial scenarios.

And so we opened an office in Kilmarnock and the young McCluskey was a great star, one of our best performers and outstanding company. We took in another partner, Des Browne, in Kilmarnock as serious talent with an ironic sense of humour and very much his own man. He became successfully involved in politics and I think reached cabinet or shadow cabinet rank.

But before that I received a telephone call from McCluskey . . . not the courtesy of a visit!! I was watching *Dr Who* at the time with the children. He and Des Browne were leaving to set up their own office! I was dumbfounded, downcast and flabbergasted. But what could I say or do? They were over twenty-one and had decided. A brave face … wishing him well and saying we would discuss financial arrangements regarding current files.

My favourite partner. Without a courtesy visit. Naturally I toyed (briefly) with practising myself in Kilmarnock and holding on to the files … but good sense prevailed. Sadly I do not think I met McCluskey after that phone call. I do not know if he is still alive but nevertheless fond memories remain.

We had a lot of business in Kilmarnock before then. I used to spend quite some time in Kilmarnock Sheriff Court conducting sheriff and jury trials. One of the sheriffs there was Reginald Levitt, a great character. He must have played golf because, whenever I turned up for a sheriff and jury trial, the fiscal, a most adroit and charming lady, was aware that the sheriff would appreciate an early day rather than a full blown jury trial. Accordingly, partial pleas of guilty were easy to negotiate and that delighted the fiscal, but delighted the sheriff even more. After a plea was given I was invited into his private room for a glass of sherry. I always suspected that the fiscal had arranged a reasonable sentence in return for the negotiated plea.

I devised the acronym IOCF, which stood for Inter Office Cross Fertilisation. The idea was that a successful partner in one branch should visit another branch and write a report. This, I thought, was a good idea and, indeed, was popular with most of the partners as it does take a lot for one partner to condemn one office or the other. This plan definitely helped to maintain and improve the standard of our work and make sure that all our offices were firing on all possible cylinders. With an ever-growing organisation to fund, this was essential.

Even as our staff grew we had a night out at Christmas – a pantomime and dinner. Times changed to dinner with dancing, although not the dancing for me. We had some fun when I finally managed to persuade Terry Grieve (of whom more later) that we should open an Edinburgh office of our own. We were sending so much work through to what are called Edinburgh 'correspondents' and thought it would be more fun and hopefully more efficient if we had our own office. This caused a considerable storm. Who are these arrogant Glasgow solicitors seeking to take away business from Edinburgh firms? Well, I advertised in the Edinburgh newspapers for an Edinburgh lawyer and received an abundance of replies. In fact, two partners from one firm both applied separately and in ignorance of each other. Such was the quality that we appointed two – Graeme Warner and Jeanette

McManus (who eventually left us to take up a Church of Scotland position as a lawyer).

Graeme Warner was energetic and brought no complaints from his rivals – although when he started he must have had a torrid time of it. Many Edinburgh judges were on the lookout for any procedural difficulties or mistakes. He worked hard and survived, but was eventually poached by another firm before becoming a sheriff.

When we were in our heyday, business was comfortable. Clearly, we needed management and I appointed Gordon Banks as chief accountant. Not particularly into modern methods, he used to produce accounts, credits, cash flow budgets and the like by hand, but always immaculately.

I have never been one for detailed administration. Ideas followed by action is more than enough. Accordingly, we appointed an office manager. Now many solicitors' firms were run by a partner, who acted as the manager. This to my mind was stupid. Solicitors were not trained in administration and their job, in my view, was to be at the front line, earning money – not acting as non-fee earners. Accordingly, we appointed a non-solicitor as our office manager – a delightful man, Raoul Gilbert, formerly a senior police officer in Rhodesia. I used to meet him on a weekly basis and left the rest to him and he was good at the administration, even though, slightly to the chagrin of some partners, he said that he was so busy that he had to appoint an assistant. Beware of burgeoning and all-enveloping administration!

So much for the rise. I became more and more involved with other matters, such as the International Bar Association, and was understandably unable to devote the care and attention to the firm which was required. The income from Legal Aid became a fraction of what it was and many of our offices struggled. A combination of partners leaving, lower income and of course burgeoning expenditure made things much less comfortable.

We had also trailblazed, only for others to follow. While we had originally enjoyed a monopoly in some of the outlying areas, we found ourselves in a company of other professionals – as one would expect. It became apparent to even the untutored mind that commercial work was much more rewarding. Legal Aid fees paled into insignificance when compared to commercial hourly rates. It did not require the mind of a genius to work out that we should really be into commercial work. Wilma Wood of our Rutherglen office attracted Lorne Crerar to leave his commercial firm and start up a commercial arm with us in the 1980s.

His first office was the basement in St Vincent Street in which I had unsuccessfully tried to run a walk-in café. We then brought in another corporate partner, Robert Hynd. Lorne Crerar had a number of contacts and the other partners were able to attract some commercial business that we could not take on beforehand. The commercial side was subsidised initially then came into its own and we set up a separate commercial practice. Lorne Crerar introduced a new man, Colin McLeod, and we called it Harper McLeod. Eventually it separated from Ross Harper and succeeded on its own, just as I was retiring around 2000. By that time Harper McLeod had moved to splendid offices in the Ca' D'Oro building, at the corner of Union Street and Gordon Street, first of all occupying one floor. It now stretches to two and a half floors in that building.

Lorne Crerar has done an unbelievable job in establishing credentials and increasing turnover. I have been away for some sixteen years but Harper McLeod is now apparently ranked amongst the top three practices in Scotland, is the 2016 Law Firm of the Year in Scotland (an accolade it has received no less than eight times in the past decade) and is as much a household name amongst commercial firms as Ross Harper & Murphy used to be amongst criminals. Unhappily, Ross Harper & Murphy, as it then was, and then Ross Harper, fell on very bad times and now is no more.

My favourite partners when I left included Alan Suskind and Cameron Fyfe. Alan Suskind is a great lawyer. I recall noting him as a fiscal, he was always by far the best prepared and always knew what he was doing. I sensed talent and persuaded him to depart the fiscal's office and come and join Ross Harper & Murphy. This he did and was a great success, eventually becoming managing partner.

Cameron Fyfe came to us from the East Kilbride office, working with the estimable partner Brian Bonnar. He was a negotiator rarely leaving the office and eschewing court appearances. And it worked for him . . . a very personable man.

But it would be very wrong to close this chapter without loving mention of Terry Grieve. He was taken into the firm by Jim Murphy when I was absent in England. A prodigious worker. If he had one detectable failing in my humble view, it was that he (in common with other solicitors) insisted that only partners opened mail. Ugh! I explained that secretaries were better and more careful than me but all to no avail.

And in any event Terry was a joy to work with, never without a file and a pen even when he surprisingly became a liberal councillor.

Very sadly he developed an illness that slowly affected his brain. I remember paying him a visit at home where he would put salt in his wine. Sad, very sad. I wept at his funeral. One of nature's true gentlemen.

A law business is much like any other. It has its ups and downs. Away from the daily challenges of cases and courtrooms, you need the best possible people, a sound business plan and a fair wind in order to succeed. Looking back, I believe we did, to some extent, break through some of the slightly stuffy barriers that existed in the sixties, seventies and eighties and helped to create a new approach in the legal world in Scotland. Some thought us brash and overly commercial, no doubt, but the world was moving on and in my view it was high time the law did the same.

6

LOVE & MARRIAGE

Ursula and I celebrated our fiftieth wedding anniversary on 26 September 2013. Many people have lived longer, but not many marriages have lasted longer.

Well over half a century earlier, as a young lad, just qualified, I went to Cala Figuera in Majorca to a type of student holiday centre. There I met a young German lassie who was extremely lovely, pleasant and very bright. After the holiday I phoned her on many occasions in Germany and wrote to her even more. She seemed pleased.

I invited her over to the UK and we agreed to meet in London. I booked in at the Regent's Palace Hotel – separate rooms, of course! We went to the theatre and saw *My Fair Lady* with Julie Andrews and Rex Harrison. Altogether we had a few great days. Ursula was at that point working as a journalist for *Stars and Stripes*, the American Army newspaper. After many long letters and many phone calls, she surprised her father by agreeing to come away and live and work in Glasgow. Our office in Holland Street at that time was small, but she could do shorthand and typing and was remarkably proficient in English.

At that time there was no European Union and there was an anxious phone call with Immigration from Heathrow Airport, who wanted to send her straight back to Germany. I cajoled, persuaded and convinced them to let her come to Glasgow. I met her at the airport but I was, unfortunately, so nervous that I took her through some of the less salubrious parts of the city. Needless to say she was distinctly unimpressed.

Born in 1940 in Berlin, not a good time to be born and not a good place to start life, Ursula's father was the political correspondent for Berlin's main newspaper, *Das Neue Deutschland*. He had fallen foul of the powers that be and been ordered to stop all political activities. Her sister's husband, a Jew, was sent to a concentration camp to ensure her father's silence. Her mother was very ill and, for her safety, the family moved to the Riesengebirge, where Ursula's mother died in 1943. The family then returned to Berlin. Two years later, her father married again and, at the end of that year, her brother Hans was born.

She remembers the cold and the hunger of these times. American friends, who kept an eye on their safety, often shared their rations with the family. Her sister, Ruth, stayed on at the family's country property, hoping her husband would come back. She had two little boys – Juergen and Michael.

The family had an old yellow Volkswagen Beetle and, with petrol supplied by American friends, were able to cross the border and visit Ruth and collect fresh vegetables which they could bring back in the boot of the car – the engine of the Beetle was at the back of the car and the Russian guards at the border crossing never realised that the boot would be in the front. One night when the air raid sirens went off, they had very little time to reach the shelter. Ursula's father had a beautiful red macaw, but there was only time to open his cage door and then run. When they returned, a wardrobe had fallen on him and he was dead.

Ursula's little brother survived this time thanks to their American friends, who gave them all their condensed milk. Her father had also started writing thrillers under a pseudonym, which sold well, though his bank account had been frozen.

Then one evening, her father rushed in, grabbed his toothbrush and a little painting by Eckenbrecher of the Riesengebirge and told the family that the Americans would fly him out into a safe place and would soon come for them. Shortly after, Ursula and her brother were flown by helicopter into a safe house in the American sector where her father was waiting for them. They had had to leave immediately, taking nothing with them.

Some time later, the Americans flew the family to Heppenheim, a small town in West Germany, and moved them into a house that had been requisitioned from a Nazi. According to Ursula, they were not popular in this little town where she went to school.

In 1949 Ursula's brother Klaus, ten years older than she, was released from prison camp, one of the last ones to be sent home. Klaus had become a soldier when he was sixteen. He had very little schooling and went to America to seek his future there, sadly dying in an accident just two years later. Her father's mother, who had flown out of Berlin with the family, died in Heppenheim.

The family had no money and no possessions, but her father soon became the political correspondent for one of Germany's largest newspapers, the *Frankfurter Allgemeine*. Soon they were able to move to Darmstadt in Hessen and life became very much better. I visited Germany a fair bit during our courtship.

Ursula's father was a delightful man and still writing political articles, which were translated into many languages. He was awarded the *Bundesverdienstkreuz* by Konrad Adennauer.

We married in 1963 on a blustery September day with over 200 guests, many from Germany. The wedding went off without an obvious hitch. We had our wedding reception at the Marlborough, some ten minutes' walk from Langside Church, a well-known venue in the south side of Glasgow for receptions and parties. And how does one escort the glorious young blushing German bride from church to reception? No alternative. Obviously a horse and carriage – and fingers crossed that it doesn't rain! We travelled to the reception in style and everyone seemed happy.

But on our honeymoon in Tangier, Ursula persuaded me to come out with her on a horse. Hers was a bit frisky, so she persuaded me to swap horses. We hired the horses at the hotel but were left without escort and we ambled our way along the road into the nearest village. I got used to the horse and we turned to go back. Unfortunately, the horse knew that we were going back and obviously was feeling rather hungry, so it bolted; not only bolted home, but bolted the wrong way round the roundabout, much to the chagrin of a motorcyclist who fell off his bike. He was lucky. I was thrown from the horse and landed on the road face down. He came to protest but, when he saw my condition, he must have smiled and left. The horse made it home without any trouble and I, guided by Ursula, staggered home. The doctor was called, as there was something seriously wrong with my leg and, eventually, I hobbled home on crutches – much to the delight and amusement of my friends. Some honeymoon, ending up on crutches!

I must have been daft. Ursula has this love of horses. I was neither fussed nor bothered, but anxious to be part of the scheme of things. On another holiday, having not yet learned my lesson, I sat on a horse and managed to ride it relatively comfortably. I still remember it was standing in a controlled area. I relaxed and suddenly the horse shifted its stance so much that I fell right off the brute, landing on my wrist. I was hospitalised. I still recall that when they tried to put chloroform to my lips I protested. One tweak of the wrist by the anaesthetist was enough to halt my protests. A plaster later and I was ready to resume the holiday, but not the horses.

On another occasion, in Glasgow, I joined a horse jumping class. This was exciting and exhilarating; until my horse decided not to jump over, but to forge its way through the jump. I landed on my back with unforeseen consequences. Fortunately, once again, I healed.

For various business reasons, unconnected with my legal practice and described elsewhere, we moved to London to a flat in Malvern Court in Knightsbridge and stayed there for a year or two. We were about to travel to Australia to try to set up a publishing company, having been seduced by Fee's brother-in-law (a chap called Dougan). Ursula, who became pregnant shortly after we moved to London, had a threatened miscarriage. Luckily, there was a gynaecologist in our block of flats. We went to see him but he turned out to be an abortionist and we fled. My brother, Murray, a doctor, came to our rescue and sent the most charming gynaecologist and Robin was saved. I went to Australia and Ursula was able to fly to Germany a few weeks later to stay with her parents. I collected her there on my way home when she was as fit as a fiddle and highly pregnant.

We then moved to Gerrards Cross in Buckinghamshire, buying a great house with a swimming pool in 1966. After a few years, however, and after the birth of our daughter Susan in Amersham Hospital, the businesses started to totter, flounder and eventually expire. On the morning of the news that an administrator had been appointed, I almost collapsed and stayed in bed. These were horrible moments but, fortunately, Ursula's spirit was not defeated and, with her considerable help, I recovered and decided to return to my natural habitat – the law – in Glasgow.

I moved up to Glasgow and stayed with my mother while Ursula stayed in Gerrards Cross until I could find accommodation. I was still senior partner and Jim Murphy seemed happy to see me back. We had brought in another partner, Terry Grieve, and I think he was a bit suspicious that I might not cut the cloth. Terry was a prodigious worker.

Because I had been away from the law for a while I read, devoured and memorised all criminal law books (Gerald Gordon comes to my ageing mind). Shortly, my knowledge became even better than that of most sheriffs as I was able to demonstrate, albeit modestly.

Ursula was happy because I *did* cut the cloth – and more. I took back to criminal law with a positive relish, all the more so since Legal Aid had recently been introduced whereby we were paid for each hour we spent on a case. And I was able to spend many, many hours going to police stations at night to take precognitions, in court early in the morning and serving on the 'duty roll' for anyone who did not want to spend a day in court. Ursula's pride in me was manifest and I was able to welcome her back to Glasgow, staying in rented accommodation until we purchased a house in Pollokshields, and then another one and then another one.

Ursula survived several illnesses in the sixties. Doctors in Gerrards Cross were unable to locate a diseased kidney but it was located when we were on holiday in Italy. The kidney was removed but Ursula did not rest. She decided it was time to adopt a child. Preferably one or two who could not be adopted easily by other people – namely African children.

I managed to talk her out of adopting two, but we were vetted by various adoption agencies and suddenly young Michael appeared on the scene. The product of a student liaison between an African man and a Scottish girl, he was in a home with no immediate prospects. We adopted him in 1968 and raised him as our own. Michael now lives in Australia, having graduated with a law degree.

As well as being a devoted mother to our three children, Ursula's great passion in life is animals – of all sorts, shapes and sizes. We were once staying at Peebles Hydro when she rose early to spend the first hour of the day going along the driveway lifting snails over the road. I should have realised then that my life would become infected with animals.

First of all it was the parrots. I have no idea why she became so besotted by parrots. We had Peppi, who was the love of her life, and Joey who bit everybody in sight (fortunately apart from me). John Smith, then Leader of the Opposition, was once at our house for a party and foolishly put his finger through the parrot's cage. Within a second the parrot had taken a lump out of his finger and blood flowed everywhere. The parrots were all friendly to Ursula. Some were even friendly to me.

Our first animal was a dog. My secretary Janis once gave me a carrier bag to take home. I didn't look into it but, when I got home, Susan, aged three, was sitting in front of something. Ursula was looking guilty and, lo and behold, a Staffordshire Bull Terrier leapt out from behind Susan and, in my carrier bag, was dog food, which Janis had purchased at the instigation of Ursula. Over the years we had two Staffordshire Bull Terriers (at least), a Weimaraner and a Red Setter called Kim who used to come shooting with me occasionally.

When we moved from Pollokshields to a bungalow adjacent to the Raeside farm, we had cats galore, all of which had a penchant for sleeping on our bed. Parrots, dogs, cats – but that was the beginning, not the end. Horses were now the name of the game.

We took the children to Pollok Park, which had horses for rent by the hour. The children were given riding lessons by young teenage female instructors with voices like thunder. They soon learned to ride and I remember escorting my daughter through Pollok Park. But that was only the beginning. When living in Newton Mearns, near the Raesides, we kept horses. The garage was converted into stables and a field outside was rented from the Raesides to allow the horses to graze. Both Robin and Susan were into showjumping. I joined them in classes until my horse went into a fence, I went over it and I ended up with a wounded back and equally wounded pride.

We went to horse shows and soon purchased a horsebox so that we were able to make our own way to shows to watch Susan and Robin jumping over small stiles. And it got worse than that. Ursula decided that, while jumping was all very well, show ponies were the answer, and we bought Susan a show pony with which she did reasonably well. So we proceeded to buy better ponies and then even better ponies. Money poured out as if through a sieve and Susan went from show to show with better and better ponies.

Show after show. Ursula drove the horsebox delightedly and soon we got another one and a bigger one. She travelled to England, driving for hours accompanied by Michael who didn't sleep and Susan who slept in the back, and one or two ponies. They must have had a good time because soon our house was full of ribbons – red, blue and green, winning more than losing. And then Susan became a Scottish champion. Her mother was more delighted than my bank manager.

She qualified several times for Wembley and narrowly missed victory to a rival. By this time Robin was well beyond ponies and Michael never took to them. Then, as suddenly as it started, it stopped when Susan repaired to London. It had been an all-consuming passion for the family and I was, of course, happy that they were happy, but my wallet and I were glad when it was over.

A great loving and loveable wife, three cracking children and seven grandchildren. Still alive with memories. For what more can any man ask? What am I? The same as I always have been – a lucky sod!

7

STRATHCLYDE UNIVERSITY

In the 1980s I was happily building up a significant law practice, making money, buying ponies for the children, playing bridge and being spoiled by the wife. I was asked if I would like my name put forward for Glasgow University, which was about to appoint a Chair for its Diploma of Legal Practice – which in these days entailed a year after graduation studying practical law before being exposed to private practice.

This appealed to my ego, having authored one or two pamphlets on practice of law. What right I had to produce these I have no idea, but I suppose I was one of the few lawyers with extra energy and a surfeit of ambition. In any event, I rather fancied the idea of a part-time university appointment, perhaps carrying with it a Chair. I spent some moments of reflection on what I could do at a university.

My meanderings and ambition came to a quick halt when I discovered that the current Professor of Conveyancing was a part-time post and held by a solicitor, and appointed without interviews. I was left speechless, asking myself, is it better not to be appointed without interview than not to be appointed with interview?

Now one of my good friends was Campbell Burns, a former editor of the university magazine and President of the Students' Representative Council – following me in both positions. He started off life as a modest lecturer at the College of Commerce, but its very small law department was merged with Strathclyde University in the 1960s and, after lecturing, he quickly rose to the top, becoming Chairman of the Law School and a full-time professor.

I disclosed to him Glasgow University's interesting conduct and explained various schemes that I proposed Glasgow University should adopt. My main theme was that the university should be willing to have courses outside its mainstream, open to solicitors and charge for them. The university could make money. Campbell Burns was a businessman and saw the future. Accordingly, he persuaded his principal, Graham Hills (to whom he was very close), to set up a department at Strathclyde University to be called the Centre of Legal Practice. He then persuaded the university authorities that the chairmanship, which merited a Chair, should be held by a well-known practising solicitor.

The way was set and I applied for the job, which, of course, had to be advertised. But only one other person on the short-list was a lecturer in conveyancing – John Sinclair, who was also in private practice. He was a most delightful man, erudite and skilled, but perhaps a little lacking in that quality which, for want of a better description, can be called . . . oomph! I still recall my interview, in which there was a most friendly principal who had, I think, already decided to appoint me, surrounded by a flank of academics. I explained in reasonable terms my vision for the future of the Centre and sold the idea of a Profit Centre. This cheered some of the old codgers up, but one did ask me what research I was going to do. I was able to respond quite truthfully 'None!' The old codger was a bit taken aback, but the principal was extremely pleased.

And so I was appointed as somebody who could run a Centre, looking after the diploma and engaging in various other activities. I inherited a small basement office and an assistant called Frank Norton, who was a character in himself but looked after all the day-to-day activity with assiduity. I was engaged at private practice and could devote little or no time to any of the day-to-day activities.

I left the entire running of the diploma to John Sinclair, the same chap who had also applied for the job, unsuccessfully, and Frank Norton and had a leisurely start, gradually introducing evening classes for solicitors. For the record, John Sinclair held no rancour and was his usual amiable self. In charge of the finances was Bob Watson, who became more and more involved in the administration and organisation and was one of the greatest boons.

As it happened, Campbell Burns did not stay too long as chairman and I inherited a series of others. I had a few ideas for the Centre, some of which were cracking. One of my fellow members of the Law Society was Nessie Faulkner. I remember her complaining vigorously that she had a son who had studied economics at Stirling University, obtaining a second-class honours, and subsequently decided, as a second thought, that he would like to practice law. This cheered up his mother no end and an application was made to the various Scottish universities.

Unhappily, university law faculties would at that time not take a student who had graduated in another subject. Their exception was that if he or she had a first-class honours, they might do so. Nessie indicated that she would prefer to pay for her son to attend university, but such was the culture of the universities that everything had to be free. And the rules about these free places were therefore dominant.

This view seemed to me to border on the absurd. It's all very well to have rules and principles of equality, but should the comparatively wealthy, or those who are prepared to contribute, suffer at the hands of the egalitarians? I proposed, therefore, that we introduced a scheme of graduate law entry whereby graduates of other disciplines could pay for a law degree at Strathclyde University. A few students paying full-time fees would bolster the finances of the Law School (and the university) and would help considerably. I set about lobbying the powers that be − all because of my sympathy with Nessie's son, whom I had never met.

Having convinced the Law School and the principal, I was invited to make a rare attendance at the University Senate. The only occasion on which I had attended this previously, I had described it as a principal's bear garden attended by those with nothing useful to do. Of course, many professors are deeply principled and hard working, and contribute to academic life. Others are civil service orientated and I used to joke that some of them would never look out of the window in the morning because then they would be left with nothing to do in the afternoon.

However, I attended the Senate and put in an impassioned plea for the rights of the individual with benefits to the university. The scheme was successful and Strathclyde University launched the first course for paid students − an idea which was derided and later accepted by other more ancient institutions.

But that was just the start and my main scheme was to cater for a very different section of the community. I had started classes on law for legal secretaries.

The great secret of success is delegation. When one was as busy as I was in other fields, delegation was critical. But there are two aspects to delegation. The first is that it is not abdication, but equally important is that delegation requires the ability to appoint a first-rate delegatee. Success, therefore, lies in identifying most excellent staff and leaving them to it, with supervision – but minimum supervision – preferably unnoticed.

Our sortie into giving lectures and instructions to law clerks and typists grew and we soon invaded other cities and sent lecturers to them. The reports from some of these lecturers were very encouraging, indeed one lecturer commented that the upper echelon of secretaries and typists were as good as many of the undergraduates, and some were even better.

Now why did these bright young girls never go to university? The answer was simple. They usually left school at the age of fifteen. Perhaps they did not fulfil expectations at school or perhaps their parents were poor and required an additional household income. Whatever the reason, in my mind it reeked of sheer luck and possible unfairness. Surely in later life we can remedy the outcome of bad luck or the product of unfairness? I thought against some odds that we should have a go at providing a remedy.

But where to start? Can we provide a gateway to a solicitor's qualification for a modest typist? In my advancing years I can recall vividly the problem and, partly, the solution, to what must have been a tortuous journey.

I introduced a part-time law degree, the classes taking place after business hours. Lecturers had to be cajoled and paid. It was innovative, new, exciting and, of course, profitable.

I remember that entries to both schemes were called 'paralegals'. I would like to think I was a visionary as I talked about parachuting them in, but I think there were paralegals in America before our day. In any event, our word 'paralegals' in Scotland was soon adopted and indeed there was a

Paralegal Committee of which I was Honorary President for some time.

There was an unholy debate about allowing those without a full set of Highers (the Scottish equivalent of a cross between O Levels and A Levels) into university. It was unheard of to allow into university somebody without qualification and numerous committees were set up to monitor the potential entrants. In the event, we managed to overcome all the difficulties and the whole scheme was a gigantic success. Numbers exceeded expectations, although after a year or two the numbers fell away and we required to bolster interest.

Although invited by the Paralegal Association to a number of its prizegivings and meetings, I believe retired folk should be seldom seen and never heard, unless they're writing their memoirs! In any event, my time with the Centre was successful and not absurdly time-consuming. I suspect I introduced to the university a whole raft of profit making. Once we made our profit, I left it to the others to debate how much of it would belong to the university and how much to the Law School. I know that there were interminable discussions. That was a matter for the academics. Certainly not for me. I produced, others dealt.

My time at Strathclyde University was invigorating and enjoyable. I escaped unscathed through a number of chairmen of the Law School and managed not to surrender my soul to the university. Interestingly enough, new professors were required to give an inaugural lecture. I prepared intensely for mine, having to submit the speech to the chairman of the Law School, Joe Thompson. Fortunately, it passed. I recall nothing of what I said, apart from the fact that I quoted from *The Bonfire of the Vanities* by Tom Wolfe, and finished on the sixtieth minute of the hour. If nothing else, this impressed the principal, at that time, Sir Graham Hill, a model of a man.

It was a well-prepared speech and I spoke without notes – I suspect a first. I wish I could read it now. Perhaps it was actually a load of codswallop? It is surely better to think the best now than know the worst.

Anyway, I am now an Emeritus Professor, I live in Australia so, like so many things, it's just not important in the great scheme of things.

8

POLITICS

All my life I have been interested in politics. My very first taste was in 1945 when my father was driving the car and he had purchased an evening paper. I read to him the headlines that Winston Churchill had just lost the election and Attlee would form a new Labour government. My father, an earnest Presbyterian minister, almost crashed the car into the side of Mansewood as he grabbed the paper to read for himself the devastating news – at least it was devastating for him. At that time I learned that he, and my mother, were Conservatives. No one could believe that the man who led us to victory in the Second World War would be defeated at the polls. I remember my mother blaming the army troops, all of whom could vote.

After graduation, when staying in Glasgow I joined the local Conservative Party in Cathcart, where Teddy Taylor was the MP, and was soon put on the committee. I made various enquiries from some sources about progressing further in politics and was advised that I should stand in local politics before advancing my ambitions to the national scene. I recall being reasonably quickly selected for the seat in Carlton in the early 1960s, which was a hotbed for Labour and I would have no chance. This suited me fine; election to local government would simply be too time-consuming for a busy young lawyer.

At that time I was becoming aware of the importance of publicity and was arranging a press release. I suddenly received notice that I was no longer selected and the lame excuse was given that a former councillor wished to stand. For a former councillor to wish to stand in Carlton was risible and I knew that the notice had emanated from a councillor, a mail marketing man with whom a company associated with me was in dispute about debt. Undaunted and undeterred, the only qualities which have helped me through my life, I sent a lengthy telegram saying that the newspapers were about to announce my candidature and that it was too late to withdraw. The powers that be relented and, accordingly, I stood as a Progressive.

What was I to do? I had no election team. I attended a number of pre-election briefing meetings by the Progressive Party and was given a few hints on how to fight an election. I had limited time but a few resources. Accordingly, I harnessed the work of my former enemy in mail marketing and arranged for his company to distribute to all the households in Carlton a manifesto and a long letter that criticised the current councillor. Luckily, I was not sued for defamation. I also arranged for posters to be distributed throughout the constituency. The poster contained a large bold photograph of yours truly, complete with beard, and the caption 'Wanted for Carlton – Harper for the Progressives'. A Labour councillor and fellow solicitor accosted me and said that I really should take them down because they were frightening the children!

On election day I toured the polling booths bribing children with chalk and sweets and ice cream to write my name on the pavement – probably illegal – but nevertheless my car was safe and my name was widespread on the pavements. I fully expected these efforts at least to raise my vote, but I am not sure that they did any good at all and Labour obtained its usual thumping majority.

Some time after that, the Hamilton Conservative Party was looking for a candidate for the 1970 General Election. This was usually a relatively safe Labour seat, but was at that time held by Winnie Ewing, the first Scottish National Party MP, since winning a by-election in 1967. She was extremely popular and there was absolutely no hope for the Conservatives to win in Hamilton. It was an ideal seat on which to cut one's teeth. Accordingly, I arranged to go for an interview and Hamilton Conservative Party committee swiftly adopted me as a candidate.

But there was one problem – I was not on the Conservative Party's list of approved candidates and the constituency is only supposed to adopt someone on that list. Hamilton could not care less and, under the rules of the Conservative Party, I am not sure that I could have been stopped. Nevertheless, within a day or two, a director of the Conservative Party came through to Glasgow to meet with me. I took him to lunch at the Automobile Club and convinced him that I was a Conservative. I have no doubt that he was relieved, but he still had the problem that I should be on the approved list. Eventually, he persuaded me that I should attend an interview with the chairman, George Younger.

He was an exceptionally pleasant man, George Younger. He was later to rise to stardom in the Conservative Party with a cabinet position and, indeed, he was the advisor to Margaret Thatcher when she was in the process of being ousted from the leadership of the Conservative Party. He knew at that time that I was an exceptionally busy lawyer but who, nevertheless, nurtured a great interest in politics.

After a very pleasant meeting, which I suppose was classified as an interview, he then asked me if it would be such a disaster if I were elected in Hamilton. I replied, 'Not at all. If I was elected in Hamilton the Conservatives would have a 90% majority in the House and would certainly not miss me if ever I did not turn up for a vote.' He chuckled wisely and I was approved, possibly a first from the Conservative Party.

In any event, the election was very enjoyable. The only stunt I recall was speaking in an open hustings in the shopping square for six hours on a soapbox. I recall going to the doctor beforehand for throat pills and taking a comfort break of five minutes fairly regularly. I also took with me the Conservative manifesto and sheaves of notes, but I found I could repeat myself every thirty or sixty minutes. One or two spies were sent out to see if I could last the pace, but happily I did so.

I also produced a spoof of the *Hamilton Advertiser* that I wrote single-handedly and did not show to the agent, much to her chagrin. She saw it for the first time in its printed version. Why did I do this myself? Because the Conservative Party is full of committees to receive remits from other committees and there is a great danger that nothing, unless approved, would ever get done. I was probably being unfair, but I took no risks.

This certainly increased the Conservative vote. I worked hard in the constituency, visiting various areas, and had a very good advisor – a local councillor – called David Williamson, who was a tower of strength. In the end, the seat was won by the Labour candidate, Alexander Wilson.

Where to next? Well, the office was keeping me very busy, fortunately, and we started to do very well. But then West

Renfrewshire came up. This was an interesting seat held formerly held by Jack Maclay, a Scottish Secretary. When he was in power under a Conservative government, he introduced the Rootes factory into Linwood, which became part of the constituency and an exceptionally busy town. Yet none of the inhabitants seemed to be Conservative. It therefore became a Labour seat and was safely held by Norman Buchan.

I was approached to attend a selection committee. There were numerous applications. It was a seat which was obviously attractive in many ways and, with the right wind, could become winnable. I was not sure, but decided to attend the selection committee if for no other reason but to gain experience of selection committees. These committees normally selected two or three candidates out of the dozen or so interviewed and went forward to a second selection before the full governing body of the constituency. No harm, I thought. And I went for an interview with other serious contenders, not disclosing my thoughts, which were, 'Do I really want to stand for this constituency?' I decided I could make up my mind if I passed the first stage, which would add to my experience.

That night I received a telephone call from the chairman of the constituency who dropped a bombshell! He said that the selection committee had decided to make only one nomination, and that was to be me.

Well, I had to make my mind up instantly. Never fearful, I said yes and was invited to attend a meeting of the constituency party. In all there were about forty of us present from all sorts of areas – Kilmacolm, down the coast to Wemyss Bay and Gourock. With panache, I sailed through the inquisition after a short speech. The secret in politics is to keep speeches simple, short, to the point and with a trace of emotion at the end. The only question I remember is when a rather pompous chap stood up and asked: 'Would the candidate inform us how he would solve the Northern Irish problem?'

Well, that was a bit of a question! Unanswerable. It would normally call for a trite answer of peace on both sides, prosecution of the bombers, etc. but I decided instead to take the bull by the horns and said that I was unable to answer the Irish question. 'If I could answer the Irish question I wouldn't be standing here as a candidate for West Renfrewshire. I would have a top seat in the cabinet, being the only person in the country who could answer that question.' I sat down, I must say to warm applause.

Well, here I was, a candidate in West Renfrewshire. If I put on a good show, but did not win I could then be a favoured candidate for the neighbouring constituency of East Renfrewshire, which was then held by Betty Harvie Anderson, who would not survive another election or two. It was one of the plum seats for the Conservatives in Scotland.

I worked assiduously on this campaign and to a point where nobody could fault, with a full-time agent and many willing and able volunteers. I visited all parts of the constituency and was even invited shooting to an estate near Inverkip, owned by Houston Shaw-Stewart. I disgraced myself there by turning up in an old woollen jumper, forgetting my wellington boots.

We were waiting for an election to be called and this was at the time of the miners' strike in 1974. I went to meeting after meeting defending Heath – he had decided not to call the election and he was 'absolutely right.' So I said.

One evening I was going down to a meeting and turned on the radio, as one must do before entering the political stage to listen to any titbits of news. On that evening there was indeed a titbit – Heath had decided to call an election. So there we were – up and running and, hopefully, prepared.

At the count we were leading at one stage, but then

the Linwood boxes steamed in and Norman Buchan was re-elected and I was back – thankfully – in private practice (the kids at that time were all going to private schools and fees had to be paid).

My ambition in a way was a bit silly because Members of Parliament in the mid-1970s were not paid very well – indeed, some MPs were suffering genuine financial hardship at this time. Certainly, it was not enough to live and send kids to private school. As a result of this, the Conservative Members of Parliament all had substantial private incomes – and required them.

Surprisingly, and agonisingly, there was another election some six months later and I was required to stand again and, this time, we were soundly and roundly defeated. I remember after the count walking along a corridor and meeting the sheriff in charge of some of the proceedings. I was grinning broadly. He stopped me and said: 'So you won, you won!' I said, 'No, I lost, I lost!' He recognised why I was grinning, but I would not have done so in front of my willing and able helpers. And although I was grinning at that time, no one could ever fault me for lack of commitment, work or, indeed, energy.

So it was back to practise with a vengeance, apologising to my partners for being absent for so long and, of course, bedlam broke out yet again. Betty Harvie Anderson of Renfrewshire East announced her retirement in 1979 and the search was on for a candidate for this safe seat. By that time my firm was blossoming and we were comparatively wealthy and I had obligations not only to the firm but also, more importantly, to my family.

My name went forward for Eastwood and there was the usual politicking, backstabbing, jostling and manoeuvring for this plum seat. I was given notice to be interviewed by the committee in the usual pre-selection process at a certain time. Some decisions are not taken lightly but I was aided in my decision inasmuch as I had a day's fishing planned the day the committee was due to meet. I took a decision. I would not go forward. I withdrew from selection and went fishing.

Was that the right or wrong decision? I think, at the time, it was the right decision and, in any event, there was no guarantee whatsoever that, despite having fought valiantly in the neighbouring constituency of West Renfrewshire, I would be selected for my home constituency of Eastwood. A chap, Alan Stewart, was eventually selected, elected and became a government minister – unhappily with a sad ending after he was involved in a very public fracas with anti-motorway protesters. He later resigned from his seat and stood down from Parliament in 1997.

After missing out on standing in East Renfrewshire, I was back at work and feeling proud of myself. Of course, ambition can always rear its ugly head again and a vacancy later came up in Edinburgh West, an extremely safe Tory seat. With the concurrence of the wife, if not my legal firm, I let my name go forward, frankly not expecting that I would have a chance of selection.

A Glasgow chap for an Edinburgh seat? No chance! Yet, I sailed through the initial stages and three or four of us were then asked to attend a final selection meeting of the whole constituency. We had to give a ten-minute speech, answer questions, disappear and return for the results. I prepared the speech well. Each well-prepared speech should also be a speech well remembered. Therefore, I memorised it word for word and spoke without notes (I must have been the only candidate so to do).

I remember nothing of what I said, apart from the fact that, if selected, I would live in Edinburgh, and the one crack I made was that: 'One of my children wanted to live in the castle and the other one wanted to live at Holyrood House. I have looked at the price of houses in Edinburgh West, and maybe my children were not so daft after all!' This was well received.

I was up against James Douglas Hamilton, who was a local councillor and I think Lord James at the time, a very pleasant polite aristocratic reasonable man, was the runaway favourite and I suspect that we were all paperweights. I had no expectations whatsoever, but enjoyed the race – and one never knows. The announcement was that James Douglas Hamilton had been nominated and the chairman whispered to me in confidence that it was the closest of all possible elections and that I was very narrowly beaten.

On the one hand I was happy I had run the favourite close and could return to work. On the other hand, I realised with mixed emotions that my political career had come to an end, although it had been a thrilling time and very nearly a second career.

In the course of my career I was fortunate enough to meet various politicians of note. I was secretary of the Scottish Conservative Party for some time, which entailed mostly sitting at conferences pretending to look interested.

One of my tasks once was to wait at a hotel prior to the arrival of Margaret Thatcher, who was addressing a political function. Accordingly, all spruced up, I attended and, after some time, the advance guard, comprising Denis Thatcher and a few assistants, turned up and I happily bought them all a drink. It was immediately after this that Margaret Thatcher arrived and, of course, asked for Highland Spring Water. When in Wales she asked for Welsh water. She was some politician.

Well, I bought her a drink and also one for the rest of her

acolytes. As I was about to pay for the second round of drinks, I noticed Denis Thatcher looking at his empty glass, almost holding it out. Naturally, I had it refilled promptly and I think he was grateful.

Coincidentally, that evening there was another reception at the castle and I attended as President of the Law Society. Malcolm Rifkind was in charge of the line-up and we went along shaking hands with the Prime Minister. Malcolm Rifkind then asked me, 'Have you met Denis Thatcher?'

'Met him?' I rashly said. 'I have already bought him two drinks today!'

Denis laughed, warmly shook my hand and, as I walked away, I felt a tap on my shoulder. Margaret Thatcher looked me in the eyes and said, 'Thank you very much for buying Denis his drinks.' She had sharp eyes and sharp wit.

When I became President of the Conservative Party in Scotland (the voluntary side) after a tightly contested election with the then Vice President, Margaret Walker – a delightful lady and wife of my former professor and writer supreme Professor David Walker – I attended a major party conference in England and, unusually for me, sat near the front and listened to Thatcher speak, nodding appropriately at all the right moments and did not fall asleep. When she was leaving the platform, she noticed me and came up to me and said, 'You must come and see me in Downing Street.'

At another event in Scotland, during her speech to the Scottish Conference, she welcomed me as the newly elected President of the Law Society and made reference to the number of offices which Ross Harper & Murphy had in Scotland, hoping that she would get as many MPs! She had some scriptwriter.

In any event, I attended Downing Street on two separate occasions. The first was a face-to-face meeting with Thatcher, where I think she was sizing me up, and we talked about Scottish politics. At least she did. On the second occasion I was invited to a luncheon at which a fair number of the cabinet were present. I sat beside her and opposite Malcolm Rifkind, the then Secretary of State for Scotland.

My only real memory of that luncheon was that one of the ministers was explaining how he had made arrangements with the opposition to amend a bill and push it through the House of Commons without a vote. Thatcher was not amused and quizzed him about the amendment and, in front of us all, started to tear the poor man to shreds.

As we settled down after that, I whispered to her that I had only read that she was like that, I didn't know she really was! Fortunately, she took this in good heart.

In Scottish politics, there are two chairmen of the party. The first is the chairman of the voluntary side (the Scottish Conservative and Unionist Association – SCUA) and other is the chairman of the party, who was directly responsible to the prime minister and cabinet. The party chairman was retiring, a new appointment was due and my name was apparently put forward to be the new chairman of the Party in Scotland. I was even rumoured to be favourite. This would have gone towards fulfiling any unfulfilled political ambitions and I was given cause to believe it was more than hopeful. But it was not to be. At the last minute Thatcher, for some reason, changed her mind from the suggestion of my nomination and appointed Michael Forsyth. I can understand this and, in fact, had no real reason to believe that that wasn't, as far as she was concerned, the correct decision.

I recall Malcolm Rifkind calling me from a meeting in London to visit him in the House of Commons, where he broke the news. Despite my distaste for some of Michael

Forsyth's then views, I naturally pledged support and loyalty, which was not accorded to him by other senior members of the Party in Scotland. I later fished with him in Iceland and even if he did not favour all my politics, he admired my fly-casting – spey and double spey cast and the little-used snake roll.

Thatcher was a very interesting person as well as a formidable politician. She used to have a table at the Ritz in the corner – the Thatcher table – and I saw her once only after my near miss with the party chairman job when I was a guest of William Francis – businessman extraordinaire and a courtly, wealthy and loveable man – and Thatcher was at her table, but obviously ailing. Whenever I meet Bill Francis for lunch at the Ritz, we sit at the Thatcher table. Memories of her linger on.

9

THE COFFIN IN THE CLYDE

I had many cases before J. Irvine Smith QC, the renowned advocate and respected sheriff in Glasgow and, indeed, once prepared a special tribute to him at a dinner marking a special occasion. Unhappily, he had a heart attack and I remember giving the tribute in his absence, mentioning that I hoped I would not be making a 'posthumous tribute'. Happily I was not, and not only did he survive that heart attack, but he survived another one.

He was somewhat senior to me and defended alleged killers when murder was still a capital offence. These must have been heart-searching and anguished days. The closest I came to a capital murder case was when I was a young practitioner and certain murders could involve hanging. It must have been before 1965, when capital punishment was abolished. I put through court a man charged with murder and robbery, and in the cells he asked me whether or not if found guilty he would be hanged.

On a reading of the Notice of Charge it would have been a capital offence, but I said to him that we would have to wait till we saw the exact nature of the charge. When I visited him in Barlinnie Prison I had to break the news to him that, as the charge lay, he was facing a capital murder case. He went pale and I was decidedly uneasy. However, a few weeks later I was able to give him the news that the prosecution had changed the nature of the charge to such that it was not a capital offence and his relief was matched only by my own.

Irvine Smith, when he was at the Bar, defended no less than five capital murders with mainly good results. He was a man of quick intellect and strong personality. But his voice? It was as loud as a locomotive train when he was in full throes of cross-examination. In Glasgow High Court there's a North and South Court separated by a twenty-foot hall. I once joked that when Irvine Smith was cross-examining a witness in the South Court then the chances were that the witness in the North Court would answer his question.

I had one famous case before him (and an abundance of infamous cases). It was one of my earlier famous cases and came to me from my former employer, Peter McGettigan, who acted for House of Fraser, which owned the funeral directors Wylie & Lochhead. In 1971, two employees were charged with a most unusual theft – that of a coffin. This case, perhaps for obvious reasons, became famous in its own life-time. Certainly it was unusual, possibly macabre and therefore newsworthy. Indeed, the reporters for the trial outnumbered the spectators.

And perhaps this was meat and drink to the three characters involved: Sheriff J. Irvine Smith on the bench, Leonard Lovatt for the prosecution and yours truly for the defence. None of the parties were strangers too, nor fearful of publicity and sparring.

What happened? Well, a Scotsman called Harry Groom was living in America and died there. He had expressed a desire that his body be buried at sea and where better for a Scotsman than the Clyde Estuary? So far, so good. The funeral directors were contacted and the coffin sent over from America. It was no ordinary coffin but a beautiful inlaid American steel casket. The manager, Mr Diack, using all his Scots instincts, decided that such a beautiful casket would be inappropriate for losing at sea. It seemed altogether more suitable for the Wylie & Lochhead internal museum.

In any event, a chipboard coffin was prepared with holes bored in it to admit water. A dredger sailed out from Ayr and, after three miles, the new coffin was consigned to the sea. It went straight down and then shot back up again. It then filled up with water and finally it was committed. At least temporarily committed. As Sheriff Smith remarked in his judgement this was, 'But the first of many experiences the late Mr Groom was to have of Scottish coffins, Scottish committals and Scottish waters.'

Before the ship could move on, the lid of the coffin and a bit of white plastic appeared on the surface. When the lid was recovered the nameplate was taken off by Mr Newlands, Wylie & Lochhead's assistant manager, and flung over the side to lie with the rest of the coffin. One of the crew suggested that the lid might make a good coffee table.

So far, so good. But Diack and Newlands had reckoned without prawn fishing. The nets in that area were trawling the bottom for prawns and one fishing boat picked up a bundle of prawns and a coffin with no lid, but still containing a body.

It was decided that the coffin should be put back near a wartime wreck of a tanker where bottom fishing was thought by the captain to be unlikely. And so it was for five days. And then? Another prawn fishing boat appeared. As Irvine Smith remarked succinctly during the trial, the name of the other boat was appropriately the *Valhalla*. The captain netted the coffin and body and decided in good order to take it to the police, where it was taken back to the undertakers.

Another coffin was prepared – a pine board coffin. But by this time the journalists were swarming all over the place and the second coffin was not used. Eventually, after police were involved, the body was committed in the original coffin and sank in the sea never to be seen again.

Diack and Newlands were charged with theft of the original metal casket. The trial lasted six days and, at that time, was of more than passing interest. Was the original coffin stolen? Or was there an intention to steal it? Irvine Smith found Diack guilty and acquitted Newlands. He fined Diack £150.

I also had dealings with Irvine Smith in relation to one of my favourite clients – Barney Noon, who had a list of convictions stretching dozens of pages. He was an inveterate petty thief, but a most interesting, and slightly learned, character. He kept addressing poems to the bench and Irvine Smith was clearly a frequent recipient and someone who became surprisingly close to Barney Noon.

I can add to Irvine Smith's stories about Barney Noon by revealing that he once had a trilogy of offences. First of all, he went to a hairdresser for a shave and a splendid haircut. He left the hairdresser's shop saying that he would fetch some money from his car. He never reappeared. He then went into a shoe shop and purchased a pair of new shoes, which he left still in their pristine box. Again, he pulled the same ruse and departed from the shop saying he would be back in a minute with the money. He then bolted for a taxi. When he reached close to his house, but not *at* his house, he said to the taxi driver that he would be back in a minute with the money. Now, Glasgow taxi drivers are no fools. Anything but. Barney knew this and said to the taxi driver, 'I'll leave my new pair of shoes with you as security,' and disappeared. The taxi driver waited and waited and finally opened the new shoebox only to find Barney's old decrepit worn out shoes in the box. He was to see Barney no more. A rogue indeed, but the sort of character you don't often come across.

10

THE ALBANY DRUGS CASE

The Albany Drugs Case in 1976 was one of the most exciting dramas that dominated my life and came close to damaging my reputation. It involved two Londoners – Matthew McHugh and Terence Goodship – both in their thirties. They were found with a plentiful supply of cannabis at the Albany Hotel in Glasgow having been raided immediately on arrival after a well-planned, well-orchestrated and obviously well-informed police raid.

I discovered, gradually, that the raid was the result of a pre-arranged order orchestrated by the police and that the drug squad was never involved. On the contrary, it was excluded. I am still not sure why I was instructed, having been lucky enough to avoid being involved with really serious crime in Glasgow and confining myself to a plentiful supply of 'ordinary' cases.

When asked to go to London to meet the paymaster, I stayed at the Ritz. This impressed those whom I was meeting. I was given several parcels of money – alleged to be £10,000. Needless to say, I was nervous. The banks were closed and

I sat on the cash during my train journey home on Sunday looking over my shoulder.

When I arrived safely in Glasgow I remember counting the notes in my kitchen, carefully aided and abetted by my young children. I am a careful sod. In these days there was no law against my holding the cash, but I correctly decided that the whole sum should be lodged immediately and forthwith in a bank in my firm's client account, but it was a bank holiday so there was only one thing for a resourceful chap to do: I drove to the airport where a bank was open. The teller was goggled-eyed when I deposited £10,000 in bank notes, but I obtained a receipt – fortunately as it turned out – and kept it.

After the trial all hell broke loose and there was enquiry after enquiry. The police even checked with the airport bank after I had reported the lodgement. Fortunately I didn't put any of the money under the bed! This turned out to be the trial of all trials and investigations.

After abortive meetings with the procurator fiscal, it was decided by the authorities that the trial should take place in the High Court in Edinburgh, following numerous internal investigations arising from my complaints and averments that the whole drugs haul had been masterminded by Glasgow police. At first there was the usual defence that the drugs had been planted but, to me, it was useless to deny possession. The defence was that the purchase of drugs was set up by some police officers and that if the drugs had not been ordered by the police, there would have been no crime. A most unusual, but proper, defence.

My firm's account having been enriched, I was able to instruct the most excellent (an understatement) of advocates. One accused was defended by James P.H. McKay, Queen's Counsel (later to become Lord Chancellor) and Nicky Fairbairn QC (later to become Solicitor General). The juniors were Malcolm Rifkind (later cabinet minister) and Bobby Younger (later to become a respected sheriff).

On the evening before the trial there was an alleged meeting of police officers where last-minute instructions were given. This was denied during the trial. The drama and secrecy prompted me to employ two detectives to travel the Glasgow–Edinburgh train, positioning themselves beside the police officers. But this ploy was leaked to the police from my own office and, needless to say, the witnesses played cards for the journey.

In the copious investigation prior to the trial, we discovered the name of a Glasgow criminal who set up the whole affair. His name was Cussins and he was involved heavily with a CID (Criminal Investigation Department) officer. Central to the defence allegations was Joe Beattie, head of the drugs squad who, apparently, did not take kindly to the alleged set up. Beattie was a most excellent drugs officer known for his disguise and nicknamed 'The Flea'. I was friendly with him and indeed met him during our investigations when we were out shooting together (he was a guest of Fred Berkeley, a fellow Glasgow solicitor and a gem of a man, now sadly deceased). There were allegations that, at that shooting, he had given me privileged information. I doubt that. He did arrange for his assistant to collar me at the office to discuss the case; a most unusual situation, but this was a most unusual case.

At that time, before the trial, I was lecturing in law at Strathclyde University and had introduced the students to the concept of a provocateur – 'Agent Provocateur'. I foolishly and rashly made reference to the current Albany drugs case and this, of course, reached the ears of the detective in charge and I was reported to various authorities. Fortunately, I heard nothing further about that.

There were many side issues to the case, including the mysterious phone call from a potential eyewitness asking to see me. I was nervous about getting personally involved in anything but, on the other hand, had the interests of the clients to consider. I therefore arranged for my partner Rita Rae to accompany me. I rejected the idea of meeting the eyewitness in his club and took him for a walk along the Glasgow streets, accompanied by Rita Rae. In the event, he said nothing of any interest whatsoever but seemed to be looking for information.

In any event, after a lengthy and well-fought trial ably argued by J.P.H. Mackay and Nicholas Fairbairn, Goodship (represented by Mackay) was acquitted but McHugh (represented by Fairbairn) was convicted and sentenced to six years imprisonment. Interestingly enough, Goodship was later arrested in England dealing in drugs and was sentenced to prison – so all our efforts came, in reality, to very little.

But the aftermath of the case was just horrific. Beattie was ejected from the drugs squad and I was visited by two stern CID officers at my house, who asked me if I could identify the man who gave me the money. I was able to convince them that I would not be able to do so and was spared an identification parade in London.

Les Brown, the well-known Glasgow police detective, devotes two chapters of his book *Glasgow Crimefighter* to the Albany case. The book confirms that there had been a leak from my office. He is also decent enough to regret the aftermath as far as Beattie was concerned and thought that, despite his assistance to the defence, he was unfairly treated by the authorities. Good for Les Brown! The fate of Joe Beattie was the greatest regret I ever had relating to the case.

Brown also disclosed that Goodship was arrested on a beach with £100,000 worth of cannabis in England – snatched from a boat tracked from Morocco. He also reminded me that Beattie had been found not guilty of alleged fraud charges in the Sheriff Court.

Interestingly enough, the aftermath enquiry was handled by Arthur Bell – a congenial but obviously forceful man with whom I had had a few days' fishing. On recollection, he was a better policeman than he was a fisherman.

Les Brown also discloses that the man used by the prosecution, Cussins, a police informer and Glasgow criminal better known as David Jackson, not only fled from Scotland, but was found some years later murdered in Pennsylvania.

Brown's revelations of how he dealt with Cussins (although perhaps one-sided) are interesting, persuasive and well-written. But, in retrospect, all I have to think of is this: save me from serious crime. Yet, on the other hand, every man accused of an offence deserves the best of representation and I am confident that both Goodship and McHugh received just that.

11

ROTARY TOOLS

Rotary Tools was a case in the mid-1970s involving bribery and possibly corruption, yet the main character was unquestionably unique and positively interesting. He was Maurice Cochrane, who came to me seeking to change his solicitor. This was not unusual in these days and I secured the appropriate mandate and sent it to his solicitor.

I had not found out much about the case. As far as I was concerned, it was just another case. I shortly received a visit, in the morning when busy preparing for court, from his former solicitor, represented by Des Queen, who at that time was chairman of the Glasgow Bar Association. I listened to their pleas, but I knew that if I refused instructions from Cochrane he would simply go elsewhere. Accordingly, I was not moved and stuck to my mandate. How fortunate I was.

Maurice Cochrane had founded a firm called Rotary Tools and amongst those whom he was accused of bribing and corrupting was a high official in the National Coal Board. The matters were heard before Sheriff Stewart Bell who, when I met him in the street afterwards, said it was the most interesting case over which he had ever presided. The procurator fiscal depute was Willie Carmichael, who was responsible for renaming a prostitute witness.

There was a second accused represented by Willie Dunn, who was scarcely heard in the trial. Willie milked the first witness but thereafter was rarely to be heard, so much so that his closing address to the jury began, 'Remember me – I am Willie Dunn, I appear for so and so – that is the co-accused.'

The trial started with evidence about the opening night of the company. Cochrane had taken over a large room at the Central Hotel and had successfully invited jazz trumpeter Dizzy Gillespie and his orchestra over from America. Dizzy Gillespie at that time was world-famous. Thereafter, the trial became more and more interesting with more and more drama.

The central witness was a Polish prostitute and it was alleged that Cochrane had arranged for her to dine with him and a senior official of the Coal Board at the Excelsior Hotel at Glasgow Airport. It was alleged, amongst other things, that Cochrane had left the official with the prostitute and they had misbehaved.

And that was the first unusual feature of the case. The prostitute, when being interviewed by Carmichael at the investigation stage, said that she would never give evidence using her proper name. The fiscal replied, 'No problem, give me another name and we shall use that for the Court proceedings.' It was thought that the prostitute had selected the name Anna Grant, but in her Polish accent the pronunciation came through as Grunt. And that's what the fiscal wrote down and that was the name that was used throughout the trial. The newspapers were not shy to make hay of the descriptive name.

The whole trial was played with humour and I do recall

one of the witnesses giving evidence that the Coal Board employees were taken for coffee by a Rotary Tools salesman. In my cross-examination, I was able to say that it was suggested that, 'It was soda scones for the workers and crumpet for the directors.'

The sheriff tolerated this and, of course, the jury and public loved it. The sheriff did not tolerate so easily another offhand question. The chairman of the company had written to somebody, saying at the end, 'Yours affectionately'. At that time, Jeremy Thorpe, Liberal Leader, had been in trouble for improper dealings with men. I could not resist asking the chairman when he wrote 'Yours affectionately', was he applying for membership of the Liberal Party? The jury, but not the sheriff, was amused.

Another highlight was a toy elephant that was part of the case. Cochrane had adopted the ploy of asking candidates for employment (girls) to sit on the elephant. He had a switch on his desk that could, by means of a hidden cord, make the elephant's eyes flash. Cochrane was the type of man who could not resist humour. It was alleged that he used to ask the girls to sit astride the elephant and then ask them personal questions about their sexual history, warning them that if they lied the elephant's eyes would flash.

Needless to say, he was given many opportunities to make these eyes flash, the more personal his questions became. He also kept in his office an idol, which he called Bung-Ho, 'bung' being slang for 'bribe'. He would ask his salesmen to bow before and worship the idol. And so the trial went on and on. With all the unusual elements of the case, the press had a winner, and the public lapped it up day after day. Sex, bribery and corruption – human weaknesses since time began.

One time in court for him I had my back turned from him and was engaged in some trivial cross-examination when

I noticed the jury all laughing. To my amazement, I then turned round towards the accused and saw him putting out his tongue at me. I was not so amused but bore the gesture with fortitude – no choice.

Eventually Cochrane was found guilty of some charges and not guilty of others. He was given a twelve-month prison sentence after being convicted of eight charges of providing sex and cash inducements to state-owned and other company officials. The memory of Anna Grunt, Bung-Ho and the elephant will live with me forever.

12

The Glasgow Rape Case

Carol X was the victim of rape and assault. Three youths were arrested and a trial was due to take place in the High Court in Glasgow. Carol did not appear and the trial continued. Medical reports on Carol were obtained. The advocate depute was concerned about Carol's mental health and her ability to give evidence. As he had every right to, the depute marked 'No proceedings' and the case was forgotten. Briefly, some members of the police force had disclosed that confessions had been given. The indefatigable crime reporter of the *Daily Record*, the amiable Arnot McWhinnie, was on the alert.

The source of his information will never be known, but the consequence of his story was earth shattering. If the Crown would not prosecute, what then? Bear an injustice? The hunt by reporters was intense. Confessions and no trial? It all reeked of injustice. If Carol had been murdered, there could still have been a trial. I assisted McWhinnie with information about private prosecution, common in England, but almost unheard of in Scotland.

I was on my way home, after sitting at Dumbarton as a

temporary sheriff, when I received a message that the *Daily Express* had been trying to contact me and promptly returned the call. They said that Carol X was housed in a hotel outside Glasgow and asked if I would advise her. I agreed that I would see her and they arranged that a car would pick me up the next morning. I airily left, saying to my wife that I would be back for lunch, little realising that I was being taken an hour or two from Glasgow to a remote hotel.

I attended with some trepidation, and Carol X was even more nervous. She was accompanied by her boyfriend and asked to be advised about her possibilities of prosecuting the miscreants herself, since she was extremely upset that the Crown had not only not proceeded with the case, but had never informed her that they had dropped it. By this time the country was alive with publicity about the Glasgow Rape Case.

Not only did the *Record* report McWhinnie's scoop in detail, but the story found its way into *The Times* and every other newspaper. Once a spark is fired, conflagration soon takes over. Questions were asked in the House of Parliament. Nicholas Fairbairn, a flamboyant and eccentric but extremely intelligent advocate, was Solicitor General, second only to the Lord Advocate in the Scottish Prosecution system. He had asked for the papers continuously but, for some reason, they were delayed. He was bombarded by the press with questions and was told that he was not to answer any until the Lord Advocate (James P.H. Mackay) had returned from Luxembourg.

Fairbairn resisted as far as possible, but at one time he was woken from his sleep at 2am by the *Evening Standard* and, to his regret, answered some questions, only for his replies to be printed in full. This was, in a way, a contempt of Parliament, since questions asked to the House are supposed to be answered first of all in the House and not in a London evening newspaper. At that time in 10 Downing Street the prime minister, Margaret Thatcher, had herself asked for information about the case. She was even questioned in the House of Commons.

The newspapers pursued the Lord Advocate to Luxembourg but he, at that time, did not have a full brief on the case. His secretary, however, spoke to Fairbairn's private secretary, warning him not to issue a statement until Lord Mackay got back from Luxembourg so that he could approve it himself. There was a congregation of journalists waiting to try to interview Carol, who had revealed that she had not known that the charges had been dropped until she had read the *Daily Record*.

Fairbairn gave a full statement to the House of Commons, but was continuously interrupted, barracked and questioned. As one would expect, he conducted himself well (as a practised advocate would) but he occasionally erred and made mistakes – such was the tension. After an angry hearing in the House of Commons, Fairbairn returned to his room only to find the Prime Minister was not too pleased and Fairbairn, somewhat tearfully, to a sympathetic Prime Minister, tendered his resignation – in a way taking the blame for failure to continue the prosecution, not that it was any direct fault of his.

However, Carol was escaping from the hordes of pressmen and into the palms of the 'protective' *Express* journalists. I was taken into the lounge where she was accompanied by her boyfriend, who was an honest artisan from the east end of Glasgow. Apparently I had acted for him before in some case or other, but could not recall that. He was perhaps the man who steered Carol in my direction.

I knew of the psychiatric reports on Carol, who had attempted suicide on at least two occasions. I knew she was fearful about coming into court, although she had turned up for one court appearance but fled at the time of the second when she saw throngs of people waiting for the High Court to start. She had wrongly thought that they were all there to hear her.

Although I say so myself, I was extremely careful. A private prosecution, while it could be conducted (although there had been no successful one for more than fifty years) would require her to give evidence. I was worried about her health and her ability to do so. My concerns were somewhat allayed when I saw before me a determined woman who did not want to see youths who admitted serious assault escape any sort of justice. She disclosed to me that (as I thought) the *Daily Express* had tried to steer another solicitor her way but (fortunately as it turned out) she had insisted on seeing me.

I was also concerned that the *Daily Express* might be paying her. She told me that, while they had paid for her accommodation, she was receiving no money. I warned her that it could be fatal to the case if the private prosecution was mounted at the expense of the newspaper. I did not know if legal aid would be available, but said I would take the case on in any event, provided she received no money for the case from a newspaper source. She assented readily.

I had of course assured myself that the journalists were not present during our conversations. I rather took to Carol, having known what she had been through and admiring her resilience. She had already had a consultation with Doctor Antebe, a near neighbour of ours in Pollokshields, and I took care that she agreed to co-operate with a further psychiatric examination so it could be ascertained whether the prospect of a private prosecution would be detrimental to her health.

I recall saying, 'There is no point in making legal history if the cost is twenty years of misery to you.' She insisted. She also made a special request that I would deal with the press at all times, telling them what was happening and making sure they did not approach her.

Being as careful as ever, I drafted out a statement in both Carol and Billy's presence, indicating the instructions that were now given to investigate the possibility of raising a private prosecution. The immediate interest became intense and, for the sake of all, the sooner the case got into court the better, when it would be under the protection of the court.

I immediately arranged a meeting with the Lord Advocate's office – the Crown agent at that time was William Chalmers. Before that meeting I had engaged Kevin Drummond, an experienced criminal advocate. He was equally agog and spent time in my office researching the background to private prosecutions.

Needless to say, the Crown Office could not have been more helpful. They supplied Kevin and me with a list of witnesses. Perhaps because of the political background, the Crown Office wished not only to help, but also to be seen to help.

Being careful of the press and what I said to them, I obtained the agreement of the Crown Office to issue a statement after the meeting and the statement was drafted with their knowledge and consent. Naturally, I was besieged with questions and, when I read the statement, I received more questions about finance. I took the opportunity to remind the world that Scots law was founded on the basis of lawyers providing their services free when the need was greatest.

I indicated I was quite sure that counsel would provide their services without charge when and where there was need. These remarks were appreciated by the older members of the Bar and the older solicitors.

But the pace was to become nothing short of frenetic. I

telephoned the Clerk to the Dean of the Faculty's Advocates, Kemp Davidson QC. He was the top QC, although had no experience of criminal cases. The Dean of the Faculty is, in the law courts of Scotland, a very powerful man with certain rights and privileges. I still recall meeting him with Kevin Drummond.

It has to be said that the first part of the meeting was somewhat fraught as some members of the Faculty of Advocates do not admire publicity and I had to assure him that the statement I had read out to the television cameras was one which had been approved, and indeed partially written by, the Crown Office. Having listened to the background of the case, Kemp Davidson then said that he would offer his services.

He then said, as the Dean of the Faculty would, there was to be no publicity. This got my dander up. I pointed out to him that I would be asked by a dozen or so journalists what had happened at my meeting with the dean and if I simply said 'no comment' then Scot's law would be damaged. One does not normally argue or remonstrate with the dean.

Eventually, he saw the point and agreed that I should make a statement, suggesting one brief sentence to the effect that the Dean of the Faculty would appear in the case without fee. This would, of course, have read like a brief telegram and I managed to put in some preliminary such as, 'I am happy to report . . .' Having seen the light of the need for friendly and helpful publicity, he (against all his instincts) agreed.

Already senseless rumours had been circulating that the *Scottish Daily Express* was providing thousands of pounds for Carol's legal expenses. Now a private prosecution starts by raising what is called a 'Bill for Criminal Letters'. Meetings were arranged with the clerk judiciary and no one, but no one (obviously), had experience of the last successful case, which had taken place in 1909.

The records of the Justiciary Office were, however, good and we were able to lay our hands on all previous cases and styles. One of my staff was an ex-Detective Sergeant and I appointed him chief executive officer to supervise the taking of statements from all the witnesses.

The scene of the crime was visited and a psychiatric report was received, but subject to further check, before the trial (if it took place) that Carol would be fit to give evidence. All the original productions were taken from the High Court in Glasgow and housed in a strong room in my office. Kevin Drummond was ceaseless in his efforts to draft the Application for Private Prosecution and we were worried that the newspaper publicity would be such that we would not receive a fair trial.

While the team was a strong one, with the dean and Kevin Drummond, we had one element missing: no one on the team had ever prosecuted. In prosecution one simple mistake can ruin everything. This was probably the case of the century and planning had to be immaculate.

With the other Counsels' consent, I made approaches to Alistair Cameron, a very experienced QC who had formerly held the post of advocate depute. As a crown prosecutor he had a reputation for common sense and, of course, he knew the prosecution process well. Alistair Cameron responded to the call knowing that no payment might ever be made. Such is Scots law.

The Bill was lodged and required, before any trial could take place, to be approved. Three judges – Lord Emslie, Scotland's Lord Justice General, Lord Cameron and Lord Avonside, presided. Four days were set aside for the Hearing. My anxiety at the composition of the bench was allayed by the fact that the Dean of Faculty himself would be presenting the case for private prosecution – a most unusual and, for me, earth-shattering event.

George Penrose, appearing for the first accused, quoted extensively from a famous old Scottish case – Burke and Hare, the infamous body snatchers in Edinburgh. He linked Burke and Hare to the present case, arguing before the three judges, 'As a result of the decision, if the Lord Advocate raised an indictment, and had failed for any reason, there could be no other trial, not even at the instance of a private individual.'

Penrose revealed to the three judges that, having researched the history of private prosecutions since the Burke and Hare cases, 'in 153 years, I can find not one case where private prosecution has been proposed after the public prosecutor has initiated proceedings.'

The counsel for the second accused, Donald MacAuley, was armed with three large boxes containing every edition of every newspaper that had published details of the Glasgow Rape Case. He argued that, because of the publicity, there could not be a fair and impartial trial anywhere in Britain.

In reply to the many observations, the dean remarked, 'The whole system is on trial because the jury system is the foundation of a civilised country with the jury deciding on the evidence and nothing else. If that slips it might be suggested the whole system of justice is a fraud. Society wants to see a fair trial.'

The four-day hearing was at an end, but there was one unusual twist to it. Amongst the productions lodged by the defence there was a postcard from Ross Harper & Murphy indicating a change of address and, apparently, sent to one of the accused.

I had been forewarned about this postcard by a fellow solicitor and said it was lodged as a matter of humour, tinged with a little envy if not downright malice. The postcard was about as relevant as a bent needle in a haystack dumped on the moon and, to be fair, the defence never made any reference to it.

But not Lord Avonside. Eagle-eyed, he had spotted it and asked Hugh Morton QC about it. Morton made hints that my firm was guilty of impropriety at least by sending an unsolicited change-of-address postcard. It was somewhat embarrassing to appear in such an august court and have one's firm thrown under a spotlight. I remember J.P.H. Mackay looking at me somewhat balefully as I boldly fixed my eyes on the wall.

The result duly came out. I was in Florida at the time of the judgement but, lo and behold, we were successful in full. But that was only the start.

I quailed at the thought – a trial in which I had forgotten to cite one of the most important witnesses, or where Carol became ill and could not give evidence – trying to anticipate every possibility of where things would go wrong, or could go wrong. I had a fantastic backup team and, as is my want, delegated and delegated but supervised and supervised.

I was thankful that the trial judge was to be Lord Ross (Donald Ross, originally from Dundee), one of the most sensible and caring judges. And we had the dean to prosecute, aided by Alistair Cameron. Kevin Drummond, who had done so much work at the beginning of the drafting of the Bill, was also present.

The trial took the usual course of trials; examination of witnesses and trenchant, at times hostile, cross-examination. My main worry was Carol's health and her ability to give evidence. I was like an anxious father looking after a nervous chicken. In the event, she not only survived the ordeal of the court but, despite severe emotions and vivid memories, survived well.

After a lengthy hearing, the accused all gave evidence and some charges were, under the direction of the judge, dropped, that is, the assault by the second and third accused.

After the jury returned, one accused was found guilty of rape and serious assault and sentenced to twelve years. The other two were found guilty of a lesser crime of indecent assault and their sentence was deferred for a year so that the judge could see that they had been of good behaviour. However dramatic the case was for Carol, and indeed for all of the defence team, the years of waiting must also have been horrible for the three youths.

But what would have happened if the advocate depute had not dropped the charge and had merely continued then? If Arnot McWhinnie had not mounted such a campaign, winning him the British Press Association award for outstanding journalism? If an unnamed source had not leaked the accused's police statements? What if the hue and cry of the press had not come to the attention, not only of Members of Parliament, but also of Thatcher herself? What if Carol had not displayed fortitude and resolution?

The clamour for justice had led to justice being discovered. Scots law is exemplified and, indeed, is a rich tapestry of helping all to achieve justice. Of that we are proud.

The cost of the case, however, was rising astronomically, but we obtained a hint (more than a hint) that all costs would be met by the government Legal Aid Fund. In fact, it paid not only for the prosecution costs, but also for the defence.

The aftermath was not so cheerful. An application for criminal injuries (a Government scheme) was successful and the usual relatively low first offer was made. I forget what it was, but it was certainly in the thousands of pounds. I personally believed that the injuries and the consequences merited more. As a solicitor, however, I had to repeat the offer to Carol. She would not hesitate and would not listen to any advice. 'Accept,' she ordered. After some delay, I had no alternative but to take her instructions.

I was not unnaturally worried that if she had such a sum of

money, even if we opened a bank account in her name, she would soon be 'fleeced' by her collection of acquaintances and 'friends'. I managed to persuade her to sign a mandate entrusting the money to our client's account. My secretary, with Carol's consent, agreed to act as her mentor and guide. I had hoped that the money would be spent on essential items, including furniture for her house.

It worked well – for a while. She then appeared with her 'male friend' and demanded all the money, as she was entitled to do. We argued, pled and delayed but no, we had to give her a cheque for the full amount. To my regret, I never heard from her again.

Finally, I was telephoned by a journalist who said that he was contemplating writing a book on the whole case. Would I co-operate? Or would I even join him? Thankfully my brain was working in overdrive. 'I cannot,' I replied. 'I am committed to Arnot McWhinnie.' That was the end of the request.

Within seconds I was on the phone to McWhinnie and we readily agreed (subject to Carol's consent) that we would write a book. When I say 'we', I have to say that I provided the early details (some of which were deleted by the dean). He provided most of the background and must have pursued with vigour even further enquiries.

So why did I consult with the dean? Producing a book on a recent case is fraught with dangers from the Law Society – even with the consent of the client. My protection was that, not only had the client agreed to the book, but the draft was 'approved by the dean'. I was not so daft.

The Glasgow Rape Case by Harper and McWhinnie was published in 1983. The urgency and the worry of the case will live with me forever.

13

MEDIA

As a solicitor, one cannot court the media, but there are ways of handling them and taking advantage of good fortune. Joseph Beltrami endeavoured to ensure that he received the maximum media attention. This was important for his business because, the better known the name, the more likely it is to attract clients.

The apocryphal story about him, much regaled by his erstwhile partner, was that when he appeared in court he would give the reporter (usually for the *Glasgow Herald*) a copy of the charge sheet. There was nothing improper in this since it was available at the sheriff clerk's office. In return for this favour, Beltrami would make sure for the reporter that his name was included, albeit at that early stage in proceedings there was simply, 'no plea, no declaration'. The story goes that Beltrami would motor into Glasgow at 12.30am to pick up the first edition of the *Herald*. If the details of the petition were in it, but not his name, he would phone to protest. Whether his partner's story was true or not, it raised smiles of credulity.

A former President of the Law Society is Austin Lafferty

and he, without any impropriety at all, is a media star. I soon learned of the importance of the media, and was exceptionally lucky at always having had a good relationship with the press.

One of our tennis court players at Hillpark Tennis Club mentioned that her father was a journalist with the *Sunday Mail* in charge of sports. I duly visited him, asked for and secured a job reporting rugby. This meant attending a rugby match (usually former pupils' clubs) and submitting a brief report on the score and the game. I was lucky in that my brief style suited the *Mail* and I was retained for a number of years to report on rugby on Saturday afternoons.

In my innocence, although I could only write at the most three paragraphs, I attended the whole game. I soon realised that this was silly and would turn up at half time and sometimes even after half time. I was quickly able to find the names of the scorers from my fellow journalists, all of whom were assiduous, and there was usually at least one other there. If that failed, I would go to the dressing room at the end and obtain the essential details required for the *Mail*. I was then able to expand to the *Edinburgh Evening News* and could report simultaneously to two newspapers.

Then, with the International Student Conference in Peru, I visited the *Daily Mail* on my return and arranged for an article on the conference. This was when I learned my first lesson about the media. I had remarked, because of trouble in Peru, there were some soldiers with machine guns stationed outside the university where the conference was held. Needless to say the story was headlined, 'Ringed by machine guns'. The press love a headline! Lesson learned.

At one time I visited the night courts in New York – in itself a salutary experience. When I sat in the dingy courtroom in the middle of the night, a policeman asked what I did. When I said I was a solicitor, he nearly took out his gun and arrested me. I then hastily produced a card showing that a solicitor in Scotland was a lawyer. He took the card and handed it to the judge and, before I knew it, I was invited to sit with the judge and he took me through the various moves.

Many of those who appeared were merely remitted to more serious courts. Apparently they had to be arraigned at the first opportunity before a normal court. Hence American night sittings. I recall once someone dressed in a skirt with an abundance of lipstick appeared before the judge and the usual sentence was delivered for opportuning.

When the judge used the pronoun 'he' when whispering to me I said, 'surely you mean she?'

'Not at all,' said the judge, '*He* is a frequent attender.' Enough there for a large article in the *Daily Record*.

At the *Daily Express* I was the duty lawyer for one night a week, sometimes two, working from seven o'clock in the evening to one o'clock in the morning, all for four guineas. I retired from that after setting up my legal firm, but still retained an interest in newspapers.

One day, when I was busy at the office, I received a telephone call from the *Scotsman*, asking if I would write, that day, an article on some subject on which I was fortunately reasonably aware. I was just about to depart for court and I took the great delegation step of putting a phone call through to one of my contacts at the Law Society in the hope that he would able to provide sufficient information and background on the matter to allow me to complete the article. Who knows, he might have taken such sympathy on me that he would have written the article himself.

But the best-laid schemes do sometimes, as Burns noted, go wrong. My contact at the Law Society was either out or did not receive the message and I was left, on returning from the court, with an hour or two to complete the article. This I did from my own limited knowledge, covering the lack of knowledge with a flowering of prose.

Fortunately, it was good enough for the *Scotsman* and, not only was it printed, but the next day I received an invitation to contribute a weekly article. I readily agreed and recall fondly that each Sunday I would sit down and draft an article which I would then dictate on the Monday, revise and correct and send off for the article to be printed on the Wednesday. I was fortunate enough in being under the supervision of a most excellent assistant editor who would no doubt 'fix the grammar' and insert the occasional verb into a sentence.

At the beginning it was easy. There were plenty of topics on which I was willing (if not able) to relate, till eventually I ran out of steam and ideas. In retrospect, my greatest salvation came from the Scottish Law Commission, which frequently produced reports on various subjects requiring attention for legislators; reports so good that they contained all the background I needed, along with a few ideas. I used them mercilessly, always paying the greatest of tribute to the Law Commission. I am told that these articles of tribute were greatly appreciated and cuttings used to be hung on the walls at the Law Commission.

I had most uneasy relations with *The Sun*, which printed an article about me and another girl. This was in the late 1980s when I was Tory party president and the article appeared at a moment which caused maximum embarrassment, when the Prime Minister, Margaret Thatcher, was visiting Scotland. The story was well covered in the media and I do not intend to cover it again here in any detail. It was a very dark time for both me and my family. Suffice to say that it contained allegations which were untrue and highly damaging, given my public profile at the time. I immediately launched libel proceedings, suing them in England rather than Scotland (where I was perhaps fearful of an unfriendly judge). In any event, damages in England were much higher than in Scotland and the Scottish edition of *The Sun* newspaper found its way over the border for a few miles, sufficient to warrant jurisdiction.

The case was eventually, and thankfully, settled and, in the settlement, I signed a confidentiality agreement, which I intend to honour. At a later stage I gave an interview to a charming female reporter of the *Record* and, unhappily, she made a headline story referring to *The Sun* and getting me into all sorts of trouble with the editor.

Not long after this, Jack Irvine and Steve Sampson decamped from *The Sun* to start up a new Sunday newspaper called the *Sunday Scot* and I was approached to write a legal column, which I willingly did. This new newspaper didn't survive for too long, but I enjoyed my time writing popular legal articles. I suspect I had to make up 'readers' queries', though I certainly would not admit that now! I've always believed that it's best not to cry over spilled milk. Much better to simply dust yourself down and move on. Some may think that thick skinned, but I think it's the best way. Learn your lessons and move on.

The *Herald* was the linchpin of native Scotland and I must say I was lucky enough to retain an excellent relationship with most of its journalists. I do recall one minor story when a Glasgow man was accused of raiding a jeweller's shop by throwing a brick through the window and running off with some items pushing a wheelchair. An unusual crime. But, strangely enough, at that time there had been a smash and grab of a jewellers in London where the thief had used a Rolls Royce. The papers made hay of my remark that in London one requires a Rolls Royce, in Glasgow a wheelchair is normally sufficient.

But perhaps my greatest pride lay in keeping something *out* of the newspapers, hence demonstrating the value of a good relationship with reporters. In Glasgow Sheriff Court newspapers did not send reporters directly to the court, except in the most important cases. There was room for an agency to be set up advising two or three former reporters touring the courts and sending the stories out to newspapers, to be paid on usage basis.

Well, I had a client who was a schoolteacher who was arrested for drink driving and had bitten the policeman arresting her. This was a story and a half: 'School teacher bites policeman'. It would have made national news. She saw a reporter in the court and paled visibly, then whispered to me that if there was any press she would undoubtedly lose her job. What to do? She was a nice lassie and we had arranged to plead guilty. I took the reporter aside and appealed to his good nature, saying that any publicity would cost the school teacher her job. The guy was, I am happy to say, responsive and sympathetic. In the event, she received a fine. There was no publicity and she kept her job. Sometime after that I met her; she was sitting not far from me at the opera and, unlike most clients, expressed her gratitude.

Sometimes keeping clients out of the press is more important than anything else. And that's why we must retain a good relationship with the press. The reporter was not doing her a favour so much as doing me a favour and knew that this would be repaid.

The daddy of all crime reporters was Arnot McWhinnie, whom I called 'Arnot McSparnot', a brilliant crime investigator for the *Daily Record* with a contact list second to none. He was my co-author of *The Glasgow Rape Case* and the one who sparked off legal concerns which went as far as Downing Street.

I have been exceptionally fortunate with the media. I was introduced once to a radio programme, *Good Morning Scotland* on BBC Scotland, which not infrequently wanted some legal comment or even legal discussion with one or two guests during the course of the programme. It started at some inordinate time in the morning, but I must confess that I was always quick to seize the opportunity of attending. I was lucky inasmuch as most of these programmes did not want learned discourses with the legal language, because I did not know much legal language and was always, as far as law was concerned, a bit of a simple soul. It was an excellent introduction to the world of broadcasting.

But my big breakthrough came in television. There was a programme called *What's Your Problem?* which endeavoured to answer problems sent in by viewers and it needed a lawyer. I was fortunate enough to be chosen and was given advance notice of the subject on which I was to discourse.

I was very nervous inititally; this was 'live' television with no room for mistakes. But I got used it and they got used to me and I adopted, as it was easy for me to do, the KISS principle. KEEP IT SIMPLE SWEETHEART or, alternatively, KEEP IT SIMPLE STUPID!

I was anxious to improve my appearance and delivery and even arranged, after a few programmes, for them to be viewed by an expert. Whether he helped me or not I don't know, but it does obey the maxim – the only thing that beats preparation is more preparation. One cannot be too careful. I kept free from big words (that was easy) or complicated law (that was even easier) and at one time I became so relaxed that, when waiting to go on live television, I actually fell asleep!

Austin Lafferty eventually took over from me and he, being a more skilled performer, was a great success. But I must confess that, on the whole, I enjoyed my time with the media.

14

Court Martials – Colonel Harper

One of my fellow solicitors, Joseph Beltrami, used to brag that he had attended a court martial and had become a Major for the period of the hearing. When a civilian attends a court martial to appear for the defence, he or she automatically assumes the rank of the prosecutor. We listened with envy.

But then a young Glasgow lad got into trouble and I remember being instructed first of all by his mother and secondly by him. He had punched a fellow soldier in the dormitory at their base in Germany, causing him to fall and sustain injury. Because of the nature of the injuries he had a full scale court martial, with all the military panoply of justice.

I had obtained books on military law, which was totally separate from English law or Scottish law – although based on English law. The penalty, if the lad was found guilty, would be expected to be severe – a prison sentence no doubt and cashiered from the Army. The case was therefore important. When I arrived in Germany I found to my delight that the prosecutor was a Colonel in the Army and, lo and behold, I was addressed as Colonel for the duration of my stay. I was assigned an Army officer to assist me and look after me generally.

On investigation it became apparent that the injured soldier was, in no uncertain terms, the dormitory bully; he was strong and powerful and did not hesitate to use that to his advantage. For some reason he had picked on my client, the result of which my client retaliated or, as I averred, acted in self-defence, defending himself with a well-struck, but perhaps lucky, punch causing injury.

Accused persons were immediately interviewed by Army personnel and statements taken – these statements being available in evidence at the trial. I was lucky – and my client was certainly lucky – in that in the course of the statement he had complained of bullying and how he had been ordered out of his bed by the injured party.

In the statement I recall that he said, 'I was so fucking nervous my fucking bed shook.'

We launched a plea of self-defence. Had his blow been excessive? Was it justified? Had we made a case of self-defence? After evidence was given, including that of my client, I quoted to the hearing, ad nauseum, 'My fucking bed shook.'

I reckoned we had an over 50% chance of acquittal but, of course, I could not read the impassive faces of the officers sitting in judgement aided and abetted, and indeed absolutely controlled, by a qualified lawyer.

The senior judge was a very senior figure in the British Army. When we reached the conclusion of the case, the officers filed out and, having read up on the procedure, I was able to advise my client that when they returned with their caps on, the verdict would be guilty; if they had their caps off, then it would be not guilty.

We waited in some trepidation. Finally, notice was received that the officers would be coming back. At that time I had a horrible thought. Had I got 'the caps on, caps off' correct? I immediately whispered to my assistant but, unhappily, he was not sure himself. There would be nothing worse than if I had given my client the wrong information. Well, I was lucky; the information was correct. The officers returned with their caps off and pronounced 'not guilty'. A grateful client and mightily relieved solicitor (albeit a Colonel) resulted and a fascinating chapter in my life was concluded.

It was, however, not as fascinating as the other court martial I was involved in. In this case I was called upon by two RAF Officers – a pilot and navigator. For some reason they found their way to Glasgow and I was instructed by them.

They had been flying a Phantom fighter plane in training and went into great technical detail with me as to what happened. As training included manoeuvring behind another plane, again from the RAF, they were then instructed to take photographs of that plane as if they were firing a sidewinder missile. The interior of the plane was set up and the training was so complete that they pressed a firing button, which then took a photograph. The photographs were then analysed by their training officer to see how close they had got to the 'target'. Needless to say, in the first interview, most of the technical detail escaped me.

But events were about to unfold: they had a change of commandant who had decreed that the training was to change. No longer was there to be a camera but, instead, they were to carry live ammunition. The purpose of this change of routine escapes me, but I suppose there must have been some good reason. Well, my two intrepid clients duly jumped in the plane and flew behind a Jaguar. They were trailing the Jaguar and put it in their sights. One of them, acting as a result of years of training, pressed the button. Instead of a photograph being taken, a sidewinder missile escaped with a loud whoosh and made its way towards the tail of the Jaguar.

Fortunately, the Jaguar pilot saw the sidewinder rushing towards him and, seconds before his plane exploded, managed to eject himself, coming to land in a German haystack. Evidence showed that the farmer's wife heard an explosion and saw a parachuting figure come towards the farm.

'Gott in himmell!' she exclaimed, fearing a third World War had started.

There were two accused, the pilot and the navigator, and since there could possibly be a conflict of interest, I decided to instruct counsel to appear for one of them.

John McCluskey, who was my favourite counsel, and would have relished the opportunity, unfortunately was not available. But help was at hand. John Smith, later to become Leader of the Labour Party in Westminster, was available and up for the task. We flew to Wildenrath in Germany and were greeted warmly.

Somewhat to my chagrin, because John Smith was a counsel, he was allocated better quarters than me. Solicitors and advocates (barristers) have always been treated differently. I used to complain that advocates had better accents than we humble solicitors and were sometimes thought to have bigger brains! I took with me a qualified assistant, Eddie Kelly, whose job was to look after us and pay the bills and remind me to have the case certified as being one of unusual difficulty and complexity (which made a significant difference to the amount we could invoice). We were escorted to see the Phantom and I still recall John Smith, with his reasonable girth, trying in vain to make himself comfortable in the pilot's seat. It was an awesome plane and frightening even to behold.

We had mastered our brief and decided on the appropriate approach to all the witnesses. Most of the evidence was not in dispute. It was not in dispute that our sidewinder missile had found itself up the arse of a Jaguar with devastating consequences.

The matter received worldwide attention. Some of the sessions required to be conducted in private without the press and we trespassed on military secrets. The essence of the defence was that no masking tape had been put on to the button that formerly had operated a camera and now operated a live missile. And we made the most of that.

When the summing up came out, I had spoken very well, but John Smith's summing up was described by a qualified assessor as the best speech before a court martial that he, in his long career, had ever heard. I thought I had done rather well, but no plaudits for me!

To shoot down a friendly Jaguar was a serious matter and could have resulted in imprisonment and certainly expulsion from the service. In the event, the pilot and navigator were found guilty of a much less serious offence and severely repri-manded. This meant that they could continue in the service and were (as we were) mightily relieved.

I bought pictures of the Phantom and the Jaguar which hung on the walls of the office for quite some time, a reminder of our trip to Germany. I never heard anything further from the two grateful clients, but I am sure that they did not, and would not, shoot at any other friendly planes.

15

MORE TRIALS &
TRIBULATIONS

'How can you appear for somebody in a criminal court and go to trial if you know that person is guilty?' A frequently asked question by those who simultaneously aver the importance of justice. The answer, of course, lies in the interpretation of the word 'know!' 'Know' does not mean 'suspect'. It signifies certainty and that is a scarce commodity. Truth can be difficult to discover – all the more so when there is conflicting evidence and a sophisticated legal system.

I recall my partner, Terry Grieve, attending on duty at court one day. A man had been charged with assault and said he was guilty of the assault. Terry naturally, and certainly not improperly, gave notice to the Crown that the man was pleading guilty and he was duly arraigned before the court. Some days later, I arranged to appear.

Fortunately, I visited the client with an abundance of

time in the cells so that I could obtain information to help mitigate sentence. It was clear to me, when he explained what had happened, that a plea of self-defence was open to him and he was not aware of that. With some difficulty, I managed to have the plea of guilty withdrawn. The man eventually went to trial and was acquitted by a jury, and it certainly highlighted the dangers of 'knowing a man is guilty'.

If a person denies the offence, then of course it is up to the Crown to prove beyond reasonable doubt that he is guilty. That is the beginning and the end of the matter. The position, however, becomes more complicated if the accused says that he is guilty but still wishes to go to trial. Then there are difficulties and constraints.

The first difficulty is to establish to one's satisfaction that the plea of guilty is genuine, rather than brought about by a force of circumstances, such as threats, say from co-accused. If the admission, however, is genuine but the accused insists on going to trial, then the defence lawyer is circumscribed in the way he conducts the trial. He may not, for instance, challenge the veracity of prosecution witnesses and he may not lead the accused to give evidence on his own behalf in which he denies the charge. I have only had this once in the High Court and, not unnaturally, the trial was brief and the accused was found guilty. I personally thought that his motive was that he would rather be found guilty by a jury than admit guilt – for some purpose of his own.

A jeweller was accused of faking a robbery and taken to the High Court where John McCluskey appeared for me. There was some evidence against the jeweller, but he denied vigorously the charge. John McCluskey, after giving a magnificent (as usual) address to the jury, left for holiday. But the jury returned a verdict of guilty and his junior gave a plea of mitigation. His co-accused, against whom the evidence was approximately the same, was acquitted.

I still remember visiting Sandland, the accused jeweller, in the cells before he was taken to prison. He took from his wrist a gold watch, which must have weighed half a pound or more, and various items of expensive jewellery. I was a bit nervous taking them home and putting them in the safe. McCluskey was furious. We immediately appealed the case and he addressed the Appeal Court. He then addressed them again and again and again and I suspect by his vigour reduced them to ashes and Sandland was finally acquitted.

This case was in sharp contrast to the Black Hill wedding reception. After what I recall was a mixed marriage, the parties went to a house and a fracas broke out. The wedding cake was stuffed in the toilet. The police were eventually called and a priest was seen escaping through a toilet window. I was given a complicated defence and required to put to one lady that the person involved in the fracas was someone whom she 'fancied'. I still remember being told by the lady in no uncertain terms, 'Listen, son, when you get to my age, I fancy no one and no one fancies me.' The fracas was so fierce that in the middle of the trial I said that this did not sound like Black Hill but Boot Hill.

Mohammad Siddique was a different character. He had practiced as a doctor and, after some complaint or other, was charged with practicing without being medically qualified. Many of his patients stood by him and said that he was a good doctor.

He was from Pakistan and told me in no uncertain terms that he had qualified as a doctor there. We searched high and low, contacting various Pakistan universities, but all to no avail. On the evidence against him I had to advise him that he perhaps had little chance of success, since he could not show that he was in fact a doctor.

He did not appear for the trial and the case received an entry in *Punch*. What happened was that he had attempted on the morning of the trial to swallow a razor blade and was immediately taken for emergency treatment to hospital. The Fiscal was Jimmy Tudhope, who was a forceful and energetic prosecutor. He had been looking forward to the case and was aghast that it would have to be continued. He finally burst out in court that, 'to avoid appearing in court by attempting suicide by swallowing a razor blade was a contempt of court'. A novel definition of contempt of court that made the columns of *Punch*.

I had two separate and unrelated poaching, or alleged poaching, cases. The first was a ghillie from the Tay, Alex Horne, who I am sorry to say was a well-known foul-hooker of salmon. When business was bad for his client he could adroitly throw in a shrimp hook without the shrimp. Using a lead weight, he let it travel to the bottom and knew the salmon there well enough to lift his rod and hook a salmon. He had been suspected for some time and some river watchers were sent to spy on him when he was fishing with some Swiss clients. He vehemently denied these particular charges (of course I did not ask him if he had foul-hooked any other salmon). The Swiss fishermen were also charged.

The trial was intense. The Swiss had taken a video of Alex Horne fishing. The evidence of the river watchers was quite clear but, fighting through thick and thin and leading evidence, I secured the acquittal of the bold Horne.

It was later, when I was fishing with another boatman that the salmon jumped nearby. I said in jest, 'That's not a salmon, that's a herring.'

'Listen, Ross', he said, 'if you were in court you could prove that that was in fact a herring!'

Alex Horne was a great character, although he had this

unfortunate habit of making sure his guests were kept happy by means of his adroit foul hooking. Indeed, one of my friends, who shall be nameless, used to be in the boat and play the fish which he had foul-hooked, never noticing that they were foul-hooked since Horne could adroitly unhook the fish from the body and make a mark with his pen knife in the jaws. Nevertheless, he behaved himself when I was fishing with him and used to come to the house where we were staying and kept ordering my young son to disclose where I kept the cigar box. He, of course, complied and every time Alex visited us, a cigar or two disappeared to the grateful ghillie.

But the daddy of them all was Peter Anderson. He was a world-class fly-caster, having won with an old, but trusty, rod a World Fly Fishing Championship, given to the man who can cast the longest distance. Several times he was my guest on the River Tay and I learned a lot about fly-casting from him. Paradoxically, when he was up with me, he preferred to fish with the worm rather than the fly.

Be that as it may, one time out of season, which means it must have been after November (the close of the season's fishing on the Tweed) he was stopped by the police with half a dozen or more salmon in his boot. He was accused of poaching them and his defence was that he had innocently purchased them, not knowing that they were out of season and not knowing that they had clearly been foul-hooked. The police found evidence of foul-hook marks on the fish. Luckily for Peter Anderson, the police, having examined the fish, decided to destroy them – although it was alleged that they may have eaten them! We proceeded to trial at Peebles Sheriff Court.

Now under the law of Scotland it is important that evidence be retained – especially since it should (a) be open for examination by the accused's representatives and (b) be produced in court. Now the evidence against Peter Anderson was destroyed. The sheriff, I remember, upbraided me for suggesting that the salmon be brought to court. She pointed out that it was a bright sunny day and the smell of the salmon in the heat would have made her court sitting impractical, if not impossible.

My pleas fell on deaf ears. Anderson was found guilty of foul-hooking the salmon. I personally do not believe that he did that himself, but it was quite possible that in purchasing them he could have taken more care. Nevertheless, he was found guilty and, of course, for a world fly-casting champion to be found guilty of poaching made headline after headline.

An appeal was immediately entered and the young Michael Ancram (now 13th Marquess of Lothian, former Conservative MP and member of the shadow cabinet) appeared for me and gave an appropriate submission to the appeal court. Anderson was acquitted on appeal. He gave me his rod with which he had won the world championship. I still have it, even after my multiple travels from Glasgow to Perth, Scotland to Perth, Australia. Not that it is of particular use, apart from its pedigree. I must confess I liked the man a lot and, as my fly-casting improved, I mentally paid tribute to him.

I dislike strongly the 'holier than thou' attitude. It was Charles Kingsley who said, 'He did not know that a keeper is only a poacher turned outside in and a poacher a keeper turned inside out.'

16

JUDGES & SHERIFFS

Now I cannot claim that I have had over my life the respect of judges – apart from a handful. When I was young in practice I suspect I was a 'young upstart' and at the time was perhaps going too far too soon. When I started life in the law, judges were gods and did not need to retire. There were some judges therefore still sitting in their eighties.

My first experience of judges as a youngster was when I attended an appeal court where three judges sat in majesty listening (or appearing to listen) to some earnest advocate. The first appeal I saw related to a capital murder charge and it was clearly of some importance – to the accused at least. As counsel advanced argument after argument I noticed a servitor behind the judges giving them a piece of paper. They appeared to write comments on the paper and passed it along the line.

I recall asking the Edinburgh solicitor beside me, 'What on earth are they doing? Have they started to write their judgement?'

'No,' I was told. 'They are ordering their lunch.' I was starting to learn.

The first Lord President when I started law was Lord Clyde, a second or third generation judge, but I never really met him or remembered him, apart from seeing him sitting grim-faced on the bench. I came across Lord Gibson, the Chairman of the Land Court, indirectly. The reason? I was part of a committee supporting his nomination when he was persuaded to stand as Lord Rector for Glasgow University. One of the main streets leading down from the Union is called Gibson Street and for many years this carried the whitewashed lettering 'Lord' before its name. I suspect that the sands of time have rubbed that away.

Lord Emslie became the Lord President and, despite his Glasgow High School and Glasgow University upbringing, was as well-spoken as the next – if not better. After I had been preaching 'revolution, not reform', in connection with sheriff court fees (which Lord Emslie selected) he asked me to come and see him. This was during some reception and, to my discredit, I did not recognise him – but after being informed by a well-wisher, I knew I had to bow and scrape.

Frank Hamilton (who reminded Lord Emslie that he was a fellow student at university) and I attended the great man in his Chambers. I am not sure whether we got very far, but we made our point in no uncertain terms. Throughout my life I have always resisted being intimidated; each man has to go to the toilet like everyone else.

My inadvertent *bête noir* was Lord Avonside, formerly Ian Shearer, who was, to all appearances, a veritable bully. Everyone quailed before him. We were at the Glasgow High Court on one occasion when Lord Avonside started to address questions to the then advocate depute (Hugh Morton). He was asking

Morton about evidence which had emerged the day before and seeking clarification – as he was entitled to do. Never one to resist a wisecrack, I whispered up to Morton when he was near the end of his reply to the questions of the judge, 'Do we have the right to cross-examine you?' My wisecrack fell on deaf ears but I was foolish enough to repeat it once again, glimpsing the glimmer of a smile from the reluctant Morton.

The next thing I knew I was hearing the words, in a stentorian voice, 'Young man!' Lord Avonside was looking down and I assumed he was addressing the man in the dock and turned round to see what he had been doing. Suddenly, I realised that Lord Avonside was addressing me – a view corroborated by the fact that some five or six counsel sitting round the desk representing a number of accused had shifted some yards away. I was sitting very much alone at the counsel's table, some feet before and under Lord Avonside. I rose somewhat shakily to my feet to be suitably and publicly admonished.

Lord Wheatley was a doyen of the bench. His father was a politician, as Wheatley was too. He was in the evening of his career. I was starting out, but there was one occasion when I was called to Lord Emslie's room in Edinburgh. He was accompanied by Lord Wheatley and I was to give evidence of a Glasgow Bar Association complaint about a sheriff, Francis Middleton, of which more later. To be alone with the two top judges could, of course, be a slightly unnerving experience and it unnerved me – especially when everything I said caused raised eyebrows and looks of incredulity and nods of incomprehension.

My favourite judge was Lord Ross – Donald Ross from Dundee – who did not assume the puffed importance of the Edinburgh alleged elite. He was a good honest down-to-earth man with a rapid legal brain and an understanding of mankind. Would that all were like him.

Nowadays, to be fair, judges are very different animals. They no longer pretend to be the gods which they aren't and relate more to human beings (which they are).

J.P.H. Mackay was of course the daddy of them all. I knew him well when he was an advocate who become a judge and later became, at Thatcher's request, Lord Chancellor. He was a deeply religious man at times and I never noticed any sense of hypocrisy.

Further, in my wisdom I regretted that many judges had not taken part in criminal cases (except those who had been advocate deputes acting for the prosecution). I always thought this was a default in the system and I took it upon myself, since I controlled many criminal cases, to instruct J.P.H. Mackay in a number of criminal trials (and he was majestic). Indeed, I recall the first time I used him, the accused intimated at the last minute that he wished to plead guilty. Mackay would not merely accept such an offhand plea, but went into the case in some detail with the accused to satisfy himself that the accused was not merely pleading guilty for convenience, but pleading guilty because he was guilty. Such care is not shown by many.

It was J.P.H. Mackay, when he was Dean of the Faculty, who intervened successfully in our campaign against Sheriff Middleton. He was also the counsel in the Albany Drugs trial. When his client was acquitted, I did detect a very slight look of temporary satisfaction. Perhaps all the more so since Fairbairn's client was convicted. Surely not? He is too decent a man for that. If one might have put one's life in danger for the sake of another man, J.P.H. Mackay would be my first choice; probably my only choice.

But how about sheriffs? Like everything else, there were good sheriffs and bad sheriffs. One prefers to remember the good. I remember Sheriff Norman McLeod, who became Sheriff Principal. He used to sit as a temporary sheriff in

Glasgow and I was struck by his manners and articulation. I recall instructing him in a number of high court cases. He was always meticulous. He was also always most approachable and, indeed, I remember visiting him in his house by a lake and being entertained royally by him.

The sheriff to whom I was closest was Sheriff Inglis, who was a son of a Sheriff Inglis of Glasgow. He did not retire till he was over eighty. The old father Sheriff Inglis remarried in his eighties and always looked a worn out old figure. His son Robert remembers slipping him a packet of contraceptives at the wedding – no doubt unused and unnecessary!

Peter McNeil was a very interesting Glasgow sheriff. He looked unapproachable when he sat on the bench, but I met him once at a party and he turned out to be precisely the opposite; approachable, social and witty; so much so that we got to know him quite well. When I told him I was going fishing to Stanley in Perthshire, he remarked that this area was famous for its hedgehogs and disclosed that he had always wanted a hedgehog in his garden.

'Sheriff, say no more,' I replied.

When we were about to leave Stanley and I asked my irrepressible son Michael if he could find a hedgehog in the garden, thinking that I could say that at least I had tried. Lo and behold, Michael duly returned with a hedgehog, which I put into a box and into the car! On returning home I phoned Peter McNeil, but he was not a former advocate and sheriff for nothing. He said he would phone me back and I later found out that he was consulting all the legal authorities to see if it was legal to transport a hedgehog! How many people have done that? However, he found nothing untoward and I proudly delivered the hedgehog to his house. The unhappy conclusion was that, after two or three days, the hedgehog died.

In Glasgow there were charming sheriffs, for example

Sheriffs Bryden, Horsfall, A.G. Walker and N.M.L. Walker (and that's going back a bit) and, of course, Sheriff Smith. There were also the awkward sheriffs. I remember once saying to a sheriff, 'I am sorry to be the cause of your Lordship's inexplicable loss of temper.' I must have been brave at the time, or foolhardy. I was lucky inasmuch as my relationships with sheriffs were, on the whole, very good and that's because, in less exceptional circumstances, I showed more than a modicum of respect.

There was a Sheriff Petersen who was addressed by Peter McCann, 'I am your Lordship's humble and obedient servant.' Sheriff Petersen is alleged to have replied, 'You're not my servant; I wouldn't employ you.'

There were, in my time, appearing in the Sheriff Court, two very difficult sheriffs. The first was Charles Johnson, who was a small man and had the reputation of great pomposity – although when one got to know him he was a reasonable man and could be quite engaging.

There was a great story that, when he went out to Bearsden as a newly appointed Sheriff Substitute in Glasgow, he was viewing a house and introduced himself as 'the sheriff of Glasgow.' There is only one sheriff of Glasgow and that's the Sheriff Principal. The rest were then called sheriff substitutes. And the woman knew the sheriff principal at the time. The story goes that she phoned the police claiming that there was an imposter trying to buy the house!

One time I got the better of Sheriff Johnson. He was sitting during the week of sheriff and jury trials and he called me in on the Monday and said that he saw I was down to take the trial before him on the Wednesday and, because of other engagements later that day and on the next day, he hoped that the trial would be reasonably short. This was quite permissible for a sheriff to announce.

The case was, however, fairly lengthy with a number of witnesses. I quickly said that our consultant, Robert Turpie, then aged about seventy-five, would be taking the trial and his face went positively pale. I added however that, out of respect to the bench, I would take the trial myself and ensure that it did not last too long. To say that he was grateful was an understatement.

As it happened, on the Wednesday I secured a plea of guilty from the client and duly pled. But there was a sting in the tail. There was a lot of preparation in the case and I asked for a certificate on the grounds of length. Normally Sheriff Johnson would have refused that out of hand but I was able delicately to point out to him in a hearing in chambers that the case was potentially one of great length and could have lasted two or three days. He grasped the point and granted the certificate.

But the favour was to be repaid. He approached my partner Jim Murphy (as one would) and explained that his daughter required an apprenticeship. We didn't need an apprentice at the time, but there was only one thing to do. One does not refuse a sheriff employment for his daughter. We are not so daft. And employment we gave her.

But Sheriff Johnson was a saint compared to Sheriff Frank Middleton. There were many theories about Middleton. He was a short man and hoped to appear enormous on the bench. He never tried to hide impatience – in fact I think he assumed it. He was intemperate and often rude to the solicitor.

Although I was an experienced court practitioner, if I knew Sheriff Middleton was on the bench I elected to pass the case on to one of my poor unsuspecting and junior colleagues. I am not sure why I protested at appearing before him. If a case was hopeless he displayed his ire. If a plea was tendered at the last minute, he displayed his ire. One was, when before him, on the horns of a dilemma.

In the Sheriff Court in these days cases were transferred at the last minute from a busy court to an idle court. I had a client whose case disappeared and it took me a few minutes to track it down to the court of Sheriff Middleton. Needless to say, without solicitor present, he had started the case and had elicited from my client a partial plea of guilty. Such conduct is just not cricket.

But I was not alone in my dislike of the sheriff and the groundswell of opinion rose up against him until it became insurmountable. The Bar Association decided to lodge a most unusual petition to the Scottish Courts Administration, requesting his removal from the bench. This was unprecedented. Of course the petition was received (I suspect gratefully) and the matter remitted to Lord Emslie and Lord Wheatley for further investigation.

The cause was set back a little by the fact that Lawrence Dowdall attended during the private enquiry and attested that Sheriff Middleton was a good sheriff, fair and reasonable. Now there was a reason for this. Sheriff Middleton was very careful in picking his enemies and in no way would he pick Dowdall, the doyen of the bar, as an enemy. His conduct to Dowdall, therefore, was very different to his conduct to the riff raff. I remember once reviewing a bail application responding to him when he said that I was wasting the court's time. I said that we solicitors for the defence require to do our job. 'So,' he rejoined, 'do the lavatory attendants and toilet cleaners.'

I quoted these observations to Emslie and Wheatley. I did receive a bad time from them, however, and they quizzed me so much that I wondered myself whether I was exaggerating, especially when I said that after each Friday when he sat in the Civil Court (which was a formal court continuing cases) the solicitors would come down shaking their heads and rubbing their eyes at some of his actions and remarks.

However, I was approached by the Dean of the Faculty, then J.P.H. Mackay, and agreed with him that if Middleton resigned we would withdraw the petition. There was an element of trust. We had to withdraw the petition and then the resignation would take place. Well, that is what happened. We withdrew the petition (to the amazement of the Scottish Courts Administration) and, thereafter, Middleton resigned. The sting in the tail was that he took up work as a temporary sheriff, but I was fortunately able to avoid him. Who says that law work is free from stress?

But I also had a home grown stable of sheriffs. First of all was my partner, James Patrick Murphy, a great and compassionate lawyer, who became an outstanding sheriff, as one would have expected. For obvious reasons I tried to steer clear of home grown sheriffs, but on one occasion my very good friend, the Rev Douglas Alexander, came to me about his mother who had been charged with speeding in Bearsden and was due for sentence at Dumbarton Sheriff Court. I knew his mother, having stayed often as a student at Douglas Alexander's home near the university. Responsive to the call, I drove down to Dumbarton Sheriff Court to find that Sheriff Murphy had recently been installed and was due to take the case! My duty to the client was greater than my own predilections and so I appeared early on in Jim's tenure.

When I appeared before him, I adopted my usual lyrical plea, explaining that how, as she was coming over a hill in Bearsden, the sun shone directly in her eyes and she failed to notice the speed. Normally I would have received a reaction from the bench for such poetry, but Jim's eyes were firmly on his notebook. It was only when I finished my plea that I realised the reason for the circumspection – half of the Dumbarton Bar had trooped in to the court to listen to Harper appearing in front of Murphy. I've rarely had such an audience of fellow lawyers!

The sentence was moderate and unexceptional. Shortly after that, Jim transferred to Glasgow and was a distinctly popular, unassuming sheriff.

Another to go to the bench was Kenneth Mitchell, a great and indeed energetic partner of ours. He was exceptionally hard-working and dedicated to the civil cases in which he specialised. I recall him helping, in his own free time, Donald Dewar, who had inherited a vacancy at our Airdrie office and whose knowledge of civil procedure was even less than mine. Kenneth Mitchell was the first one who took proper minutes at partnership meetings and I still remember them being carefully and legibly written out. I never appeared before him but heard good reports of his conduct on the bench, although in the beginning he may have appeared to some to be a little impatient, if not irascible.

Graeme Warner was a partner of ours in the Edinburgh office for quite some time and then left to go to another firm – despite my best endeavours and despite my obtaining for him an appointment as a temporary sheriff. He later became a full sheriff, but was on some occasions nearly overwhelmed by illness. I have fond, albeit mixed, memories of his tenure with us.

Rita Rae was another. I persuaded her to become a partner in our criminal division. She was very good, but had a totally different approach to my harum scarum activities – always being extremely careful not to take on too many cases in one day in the busy Sheriff Court. I must confess I used to hop from court to court, causing anxiety to the clients. I gather that she went on to be successful as a sheriff.

But last, and certainly least, I was for some time appointed as a temporary sheriff myself. I am not sure just how this strange appointment took place, but I could not resist it, buying a wig for the purpose. Temporary sheriffs are called out on a day-to-day basis to assist a court which needs help. Obviously, I could not appear in the courts in which we had offices, and they certainly numbered Glasgow, Edinburgh, Ayr, Kilmarnock, Airdrie and others. Dumbarton was free from Ross Harper & Murphy depredations and was a reasonable distance from Glasgow. That was my favourite location.

I always regarded acting as a sheriff (where there was a payment of some sorts) as a day off; something different. In the early days I would go into the office first and rush down to the court to be there before 10am. I suspect I did not keep this up for too long. Dumbarton was one of my favourite places. I knew the sheriff clerk – John Doig – well, and his very presence there made sure that I was always on time. One of the virtues of Dumbarton for me was that, at lunchtime, the other sheriffs – including Jim Murphy – appeared for lunch at some nearby hotel and, if I had any problems on that day, I could freely discuss them with my betters.

For obvious reasons I confined myself to criminal courts. I do not think I was ever called on to do a sheriff and jury and therefore my tasks related to summary work with a maximum prison sentence at that time of six months. Not that I sent anyone to prison – apart from one. I still recall the case, although not the location. A motorist had been guilty of dangerous driving, resulting in a death. The fiscal service was treating this as important and, indeed, the head fiscal, unusually, attended the summary court. The miscreant (who had a number of previous convictions) had a period in jail, but I must confess I did not feel any the better for it.

At one time I landed up in Perth and expected the usual conglomeration of summary crime. I was somewhat taken aback to be told that I had been allocated a civil debate. Now debates take place prior to a proof of one of the parties in the civil litigation and explore with matters of relevance, competence and other archaic matters. Before going to the bench I was given a copy of the closed record (that is the written pleadings) and I saw, to my distress, reference in the pleadings to a 'dominant tenement'. Now my knowledge of tenements was confined to old Glasgow buildings, but I do not think that was what was meant. Nevertheless, somewhat nervous but endeavouring to appear confident, I went on the bench and listened to a Perth solicitor and an Edinburgh counsel appearing for the other side. After about an hour of 'learned' debate in which I suspected the solicitor did not know much more about it than I did, I decided to use the sheriff's prerogative and decreed a brief ten-minute recess. During that time I scrabbled through every available book to come to terms with the exact meaning of 'dominant tenement'.

The other side instructed counsel, who was well prepared and articulate. The debate lasted into the afternoon and I was left with copious notes and a requirement to issue a written judgement. Help ma boab! What to do? There was only thing for me to do: gird up the loins and seek assistance. Well, request humbly for assistance.

And where better to go than my former partner, sitting sheriff and lawyer supreme, James Patrick Murphy? I poured out my heart to him about dominant tenements and he agreed to look at the matter. So I sent him papers, my notes and anything that might help him.

He was a star. He was a genius. He saved my life and not only helped me form a view, but thereafter wrote an immaculate judgement of which the Lord President himself would have been proud. I had the judgement typed and signed and sent to Perth. Hopefully never again. But the success of J.P. Murphy had a sting in the tail – both sides requested my attendance for the proof. Ouch! But I was lucky (the story of my life!). Both parties had, before the proof, reached an agreement. The case was settled and, as far as I concerned, dominant tenements became dust. To my discredit, I still have no idea as to what in law a dominant tenement is.

I must confess that my sense of humour never left me, even when on the bench, but not always to good effect. I was once sitting at Paisley Sheriff Court and got landed with an avalanche of cases where TV licences had not been paid and all of which required individual determinations. It was going to be a wearisome couple of hours on the bench and when one of the first cases involving TV licences came up I could not resist the quip of asking the fiscal, 'Can I endorse the licence?' Endorsement takes place in driving offences where driving licenses can be endorsed.

I think the fiscal took the question in good part, but I recall the poor sheriff clerk sitting in front of me taking assiduous notes jumping up with an alarmed face saying *sotto voce*, but heard throughout the court I am sure, 'Sheriff, sheriff, you cannot do that!' I thanked him and we proceeded – at least I had a struck a blow for something, perhaps for not taking everything too seriously even when you're on the bench.

17

LIFE AT THE TOP

When we started up in law, there was founded a Glasgow
Bar Association (GBA) which became a thorn in the flesh of
the authorities. Harry Flowers, now deceased, used to remark
that what the Law Society needed was 'ginger in the suet
pudding'. At one time, because of the indolence of the office
bearers, it fell into disarray – a shadow of its former self. I was
approached by a number of deal makers and asked if I would
stand as president of the Association. From zero to presidency
was too good an invitation. I did so, serving not only one
year, but an extended year.

The appointment was exhilarating. I found myself in trouble
with the authorities but, nevertheless, they listened. My main
recollection was the question of legal fees, which were fixed
by the then Lord President, Lord Emslie. There had been no
movement in them for some years, despite inflation.

I recall giving a speech in which I was bold enough to
say that reform was needed and, if there was no reform, we

needed a revolution. Well, this set the cat among the pigeons. Two of us, Frank Hamilton, a fellow Glasgow solicitor and I, were invited to meet with the Law President. We argued the case as best we could, with some success.

I like to think that I was an active president in many ways and still recall travelling on the boat to Rothesay where we were hosting a conference. There were a number of visitors and one of the benefits of being a president was that one gets to meet sheriffs and influential men on different terms.

After the GBA I decided, after an approach, to stand for the Council of the Law Society of Scotland, which requires a bit of time, holding its monthly meetings in Edinburgh. That in itself would not be a chore, but once one was in an organisation such as this, inevitably one gets sucked into committees. I started off on the Complaints Committee but soon departed from there for public relations – that was different. Much more my cup of tea and a role where I felt I could make a difference. Life is all about public relations. Ask any politician if you don't believe me.

Probably the highlight of my life in the Law Society was that I was invited to become Chairman of the Encyclopaedia Committee. The Law Society was already committed to an editor of a new encyclopaedia comprising over a dozen volumes. The editor was Sir Thomas Smith, a professor of Scots Law at Edinburgh University.

I came to a newly formed committee of Law Society representatives and editors and was told in no uncertain terms by Sir Thomas that the objective was to publish all the volumes simultaneously. And so we reached a wide gap between the intelligentsia and the practical. Such an ambitious undertaking was just not practical. Indeed, it was clearly impossible. After many meetings requiring diplomacy and tact, it was agreed that we should publish them consecutively, each some months apart.

It was a monumental work, the likes of which had only been published once before in Scotland, more than fifty years previously. Perhaps to humour me, Sir Thomas Smith asked me to contribute a chapter entitled 'Contempt of Court'. I wonder whether there was a hidden significance in that choice?

At that time I was extremely busy, so I gave the task to a bright apprentice with a first-class honours degree. She sculpted the article. It was then submitted and Sir Thomas's sub-editors and professors of law themselves managed to turn it into some sort of salvageable article.

I always dreaded the regular meetings where Sir Thomas Smith would lay down the law and we would have to subtly change many of his decrees and edicts. Nevertheless, he persevered in the production and it was eventually a great success. It was dedicated to Prince Charles, and Sir Thomas even wrote a foreword for the prince. There was to be a grand opening celebration and it was reasonably expected that Prince Charles would attend. I have to admit that, despite using best endeavours and best contacts, that effort failed. I was, after the many years of involvement in that production, made an honorary member of the Law Society because of these efforts. A gesture which was much appreciated.

My Law Society days were not always so successful. I once made a speech to a society in Edinburgh (Writers to the Signet) in which I criticised the progress in the civil courts in Scotland, which lost the time of many judges to the fast growing criminal courts. The secretary received an extremely stiff, if not abusive, letter from Lord Emslie himself, who was referred to by some as E.M. Sly! And he did not pull his punches about my speech, which 'most seriously found its way into the press'. This, of course, was because we had a good public relations department!

I knew that my fellow officers would instinctively side with the revered Lord President himself. I did, however, have a ploy. I showed them a copy of the speech and, although perhaps it was stronger than they would have dared, they took no exception to it. Once the speech was accepted the rest was easy. I then produced a copy of the letter from Lord Emslie (chairmen have certain powers) and they, having already approved my speech, could do nothing other than disapprove of the letter. In any event, some of the officers were despatched. No more was heard of the matter.

Being a natural rebel, I had many more run-ins. The presidency was only for a year, however, and passed quickly, although I made the mistake of drawing up a programme in the dying weeks of my presidency. But the man who never makes mistakes never makes anything. It was an honour to be a president of the Law Society, an honour of which, up until the year before I became president, was honoured by the Queen, usually with an OBE. The rules were changed, though I did not worry, since I was already a CBE.

The highlight of my 'public service' came through the International Bar Association. I did not know much about this body, but attended a meeting in Amsterdam on office technology. I was not quiet at that meeting, as I rarely am, and was invited to serve on various subcommittees of the IBA, and was eventually to stand as secretary of what was then called the Section of General Practice (SGP). The vice president was John Buckley and there was within the IBA sections *cursus honarium*, whereby the vice president became the president, or rather chairman. The secretary became the vice chairman – other things being equal.

We had an unusual chairman when I was secretary – an American who had many odd ideas. John Buckley was the vice chairman. He was from Ireland and became a very good friend. He still is.

Progression in life is much to do with luck. I wasn't sure that I fancied becoming vice chairman for two years and then chairman for another two years. Time is too short. John Buckley had, however, other fish to fry and decided that he would not stand as chairman when it was his turn and would delay. The way was therefore open for me to stand for, and be elected as, chairman without first being in the vice position. This entitled me to sit on the management committee, which entitled me to move within the powers of influence. Which I did. Vaulting ambition.

After my two years as chairman of the SGP was finished, I decided to stand as vice president of the IBA. I was duly elected vice president and then, after some scares, became president in 1995. The main scare was when a section of business law was about to support a woman candidate from Australia. She was very popular and, indeed, very good, although she antagonised some African and Asian potential voters with an ill-advised comment during a meeting.

In any event, fortune lies in our stars and, would you believe it, this lady, who would in all probability have beaten me in the election, was appointed a judge in Australia. With the collapse of my opponent, I sailed into the position, lasting almost two years from 1995 to 1996.

This took us to London and I was able to visit the IBA headquarters where the outgoing secretary was Madeleine May. I hope she did not leave because of me. She probably felt that her time to bow out on a high had come. The new secretary/chief executive was Paul Hoddinot, a former rear admiral which led to some difficulties with the Argentinian Bar Association because he had been around during the time of the Falklands War.

I recall anointing my first year 'The Year of Africa' and the second year 'The Year of Latin America' in an effort to interest further the countries which may have felt neglected. After some cajoling, Paul Hoddinott had arranged that we could take a group of African leaders to meet Nelson Mandela in Pretoria at his official residence. Many African leaders of their Bar Associations attended, and some twenty of them were looking forward to visiting and meeting the great man himself. It was a traumatic meeting.

Just before the conference was due to start, Paul Hoddinott received a message from one of Mandela's staff saying that, despite the prior arrangement, the meeting was cancelled as he had other business to attend to. I verged between being nonplussed and angry. 'This cannot happen,' I argued. 'Many leaders are coming to the conference on our promise that they would meet Mandela.'

But what on earth could we do? My Scots blood got the better of me and I persuaded Paul Hoddinott to phone the South African dignitaries, pleading on the one hand, arguing on the other, and threatening as a last resort. What was our threat? I indicated that I would take the busload of leaders out to Pretoria and stand outside the residence protesting in public that we had arranged a meeting with Mandela. One of these arguments eventually worked and the advisors relented and confirmed (thank goodness) that the meeting would take place, though it would be relatively short. I was pleased beyond belief. I would have found it very difficult to face the African Bar leaders who had attended on what might have been a false premise. So a bus was booked and we ladled into it.

We duly trundled there and were greeted in beautiful weather in an equally beautiful garden. Drinks were dispensed and the great man came out in his customary shirtsleeves. I was able to take him round the delegation and introduce him to all those taking part. They were exceptionally impressed. When somebody announced from which country he was from, Mandela would immediately say 'Oh yes, I know your President So and So – have you met him?' He was charm personified.

One of my duties was to present him with a small gift; a pair of IBA cufflinks and a certificate. I suspect he never wore cufflinks, but he accepted the gift graciously and we both gave a speech. Cameras were not supposed to be allowed, but no one stopped photographs being taken and one was printed in the *Glasgow Herald* on the front page with the allegedly funny caption: Who's that with Ross Harper!

I had read his book *Long Walk to Freedom* and, even before then, was a total Mandela convert. In honour of the man, at IBA we appointed Mandela honorary president of the newly formed Human Rights Institute, a position which was accepted on his behalf with grace.

At the time of our visit there was a Miss World Competition and when Mandela had to leave, he told the group of us that he had to go to meet the Miss World beauties and laughed, commenting that they might prove to be better company. The memory of his personality, good cheer and depth of understanding will live with me forever.

Apart from this visit to Mandela, there are many memories which are outstanding from my time at the IBA. The first was that I had to attend two brief meetings in Seville when the privatisation of Scottish Coal was entering a crucial point. I required to be back in London for an important meeting with Rothschilds the following day.

Unhappily, there was an air strike in Seville and I had no alternative. With the aid of my host, we arranged a car trip to another far off airport. I was required to travel overnight.

Since I had been taken out for dinner that evening by my host, I had an extra glass or two of wine and slept soundly on the way back. Until the driver stopped at an all-night 'café' and said that he was going in for a cup of coffee. Never one to refuse, I joined him and was given a cup of coffee. Little did I know that this coffee was designed to keep all night drivers, truck drivers and the like firmly awake. I can almost still feel my head throbbing as the coffee took hold of me. It did not leave my system for another twenty-four hours. Nevertheless, I made the plane and the meeting.

And when in Latin America, ably and firmly guided by Fernando Pelaez–Pier, I visited more countries than I can possibly remember, meeting with many lawyers, various organisations, courts and the like. Fernando was an excellent guide and host and fancied my job. I told him that he should become chairman of the Section of Business Law and progress to the president of the IBA. He took my advice and he did indeed become president of the IBA in 2009.

At one time he took me to Panama, where the local lawyer acted for the canal company. I was accordingly taken to the canal, where I was given the privilege of turning a real lock. I turned it and, to my amazement, a large ship appeared some twenty feet or more above its original position. This was power indeed, given to the few! I felt like a strong and powerful Samson without the Delilah.

18

DELEGATION

I rely on others, but delegation does not mean abdication.

One of my best and longest serving secretaries was a girl who was able, competent and had a great rapport with any of the persons with whom I was dealing – including Ursula. I grew more and more to rely on her and delegated more and more. I entrusted her to write cheques and look after my bank statements. I always seemed to spend more than I thought, but Ursula was also a signatory to the bank account and, not unnaturally, I blamed her for her extravagance.

I was doing well at the time in the early 2000s and did not have the energy or the inclination to worry about money. My mistake! But I do remember at one time wondering what was happening to the money – made various spot checks on the bank account, but could see nothing particularly untoward. Again, I did not have time to undertake a thorough examination.

When I retired I had more time. I decided to visit my bank.

When I was a lad, cheques were returned each month. Not now, nor then. Then I uncovered a few cheques payable to my secretary with a signature which I did not think was mine. My signature, however, has always been extremely poor. I telephoned her and she said that she had 'signed' a few cheques. 'For goodness sake,' I said, 'how much?' 'Oh, just a little,' I was assured.

A revisit to the bank did not confirm this assertion at all. When I had finished my examination, going back over many years (fortunately the bank was able to retrieve old cheques), the figure came well into six figures – £150,000.

So much for my blame of Ursula! So much for my lack of care and diligence in examining my bank accounts. Delegation? Yes, but with SUPERVISION.

When I had dug out her vast number of cheques, I consulted Rod McKenzie, who listened in his usual indomitable and inscrutable way. With a witness, he obtained admissions from the secretary and promptly dismissed her. The police were called and an action was mounted against my bank for honouring forged cheques.

She consulted a good solicitor and, after looking at every angle, a plea of guilty was tendered by her. I still felt a bit responsible myself and wrote a letter to her solicitor for tendering to the court saying that she had been an extremely competent secretary (that is, apart from her misdemeanour).

She was sentenced and sent to prison. I was gobsmacked, but realise that breach of trust from a secretary is an offence which does call for, and merit, a prison sentence.

Civil action against the bank had been mounted and taken over by one of Rod's partners. Efforts were made in vain to obtain a statement from the secretary when in prison. For some unaccountable reason, she gave a statement to the lawyers for the bank. The bank resisted the claim and I recall giving specimen signatures to an expert who had been called in by both the bank and Harper McLeod. The bank finally agreed to settlement – but not without considerable difficulty and some loss to me. Another lesson learned.

19

POLITICAL FRIENDS

At a political function one time Margaret Thatcher had no hesitation bashing, in no uncertain terms, a group of bankers in front of everyone, accusing them of all the nation's ills – eyes flashing and fingers pointing. Whether at home or in Scotland, she was always in charge and, in fact, my favourite expression is one of hers: 'There is no alternative' (TINA).

She was one of the most redoubtable persons I have ever met: relevant, piercing, enquiring and eternally vigilant. She was, of course, not universally popular, especially in Scotland, but she remains a role model for us all. I have no doubt that she saved the country in many ways and I remain proud to have met her.

I did not know Tony Blair well, but what I saw of him impressed me, despite the fact that he was allegedly a socialist. I first met him at a function in 1994 in memory of John Smith, at which he impressed me with his concern, attitude and understanding. Another time I met him was at a function in

Downing Street when he was Prime Minister. I had arranged this function to raise money for a Donald Dewar fund to finance a Chair in his memory at Glasgow University. I was approached by the university to run the appeal and, naturally, I went at it with gusto, and we were involved in sending out an appeal to all and sundry.

The result of these mass appeals is usually disappointing, and this was no exception. There was nothing for it but to launch personal appeals to rich individuals and, more importantly, corporations. I received, after a direct appeal to the managing director, a large cheque from Scottish Power and, being aware of the drawing power, Downing Street arranged a special function for those who had donated, or were seriously considering doing so. Dinner in the House of Lords was an additional attraction by way of a bonus.

This was successful and Tony Blair and his wife both appeared at Downing Street. I recall giving a vote of thanks to the Prime Minister and subsequently, dare I say it, I was told by Derry Irvine that the Prime Minister had been extremely impressed. I followed Tony Blair's career through thick and thin, not supporting him publicly, but admiring a man of substance, energy and understanding. There has been plenty of flak around him over the years but I still remember him with affection and there is no doubt that he is one of the major political figures of recent times.

As mentioned earlier, I knew the Right Honourable John Smith QC well, very well. He was a year or two behind me at university and was at that time a great pal of Derry Irvine (the future Lord Chancellor). He was an apprentice with a firm specialising in small debt (Joseph Mellick & Co). I used to see him regularly at the Sheriff Court and recall coffees and lunch.

His ambition was to become Secretary of State for Scotland.

My ambition was to become a sheriff at Perth. In those days sheriffs led extremely comfortable lives and I knew that I would have plenty of time for fishing on the Tay. We had a pact, believe it or not. He had announced his intention of going to the Bar and I was a frequent source of business to all and sundry. I said that I would send him an abundance of work in return for which he could appoint me a sheriff of Perth. Oh, the folly and wisdom of the young!

In any event, I was true to my word and did give John Smith an avalanche of work, at which he was exceptionally good. I gave him his first High Court jury trial and, thereafter, he continued to act on many occasions, the most significant case being the aforementioned court martial in Germany where the pilot and navigator had shot down one of their own planes by mistake.

His widow Elizabeth now sits in the House of Lords. I remember that she was interested in Russian art. At one time I sent over a fellow partner, Robert Hynd, who spoke Russian, to assist in her endeavours. Dealing with Russian art had its complications. At one of my last meetings with John Smith, when he was sitting in his Leader of the Opposition office, I warned him about the possible personal financial dangers. I recall that he was not amused.

At one time I think he had signed a guarantee for some debt in his wife's business. Or, it was alleged that he had signed the guarantee. In any event, the creditor was an awkward bugger and was asking for payment of some money. John, being an aggressive lawyer, had decided to fight the case and consulted me. I sensed, smelled and foresaw all sorts of danger. John, at that time, was Shadow Chancellor of the Exchequer and I could see the headlines if he was sued for a disputed debt. If he could not manage his own personal affairs, how could he manage the affairs of the country?

I was persuasive (rightly so) although John had to borrow money (to which I contributed) to see off the demanding creditor. When one goes from being an advocate to Parliament, income drops dramatically. I remember when he was first selected as the prospective candidate for Coatbridge (a safe Labour seat), by coincidence in the same week I had been selected for Hamilton as a Conservative (a safe Labour seat). But he, like a rocket, rose and rose.

As a young advocate he helped me draft an important case. I subsequently persuaded my Edinburgh partner, Graham Warner (initially against his will), to instruct John in divorce cases. Divorce court met on a Saturday morning, which was one of the few days on which John could be free.

John stayed in Morningside and I remember visiting him at his house after his first heart attack in 1988 and his description of it was horrific. He had not felt well that morning and was due to travel to London. His wife was worried and called a doctor. The doctor was even more worried about the possibility of heart trouble and sent him to hospital. Thereafter, John was put through the usual tests, including a treadmill. After completing these tests, he told me that the doctor had come into the room where he was changing and said, 'You have no problem with your heart, Mr Smith. Your heart is in great condition and better than most.'

Mightily relieved, John bent down to lace up his shoes and then was hit by a serious heart attack from which he took quite some time to recover. I heard all this in awe. All I was able to offer him was a copy of *The Bonfire of the Vanities,* a great story from which I quoted in my inaugural lecture as Professor at Strathclyde University.

John gradually recovered his health and was able to go for walks in the hills. Unhappily, he had another, this time fatal, heart attack in 1994 and, not unnaturally, his funeral service in Edinburgh was crowded. Derry Irvine and Donald Dewar gave absolutely splendid orations about the great man.

I remember that one time, when he was in office in some cabinet position, he telephoned me and asked me if I would like to become a member of the Board of British Airways. I need not seek speculation as to my answer. As it happened, the prospect of a Glasgow criminal solicitor being on the Board of British Airways did not pass through the many barriers. But the thought was there. If he'd been Prime Minister (as he nearly was) where would I be now? I would have certainly lost the appetite to be Sheriff of Perth!

Gordon Brown was Chancellor of the Exchequer in the wake of Tony Blair until eventually he became Prime Minister and achieved his lifetime ambition. I remember him when he worked for Scottish Television in an executive role in the early 1980s and was told by one of the broadcasters that he seemed to spend most of the time on the telephone in political discussions. Little wonder, Gordon Brown is a politician through and through.

He once spoke exceptionally well at a fundraising luncheon. I admired this and I also must confess I admired him – not for his career as Chancellor of the Exchequer and Prime Minister – but for other qualities: determination, warmth and intellect.

Even closer to John Smith was Donald Dewar and I was even closer to him. I knew him well at university, where he was a formidable debater, winning national trophies (as did John Smith). He was a thin, angular man who could scoff a meal and clear the plates of everyone else in sight. He never actually put on weight. Not for nothing at that time was he known as 'the gannet'.

Donald was in Parliament, then lost his seat and returned to work as a lawyer. He became a reporter (i.e. a prosecutor in children's courts) for some time, but clearly that relatively lowly job did not suit his talents.

When I met him at a party, I suggested that he come into private practice. At that time we had a vacancy for a partner in our Airdrie office and Donald, never one to resist a challenge, accepted. A Conservative lawyer taking on a former Labour MP. But that was one thing in Scotland: politics did not divide friendship and, apart from the occasional comment or humorous barb, there is no way in which friends would debate the relative merits of their parties. In England, at that time, it was different.

I recall having a party in London where our bridge friends were amazed that I should invite politicians of both parties who would happily socialise together. In fact, I am sure Derry Irvine (Labour) made John Mackay (Conservative) inebriated during one of my parties with, of course, my finest wine.

In any event, Donald Dewar, who had never really engaged in any private practice, did shine in the criminal courts and employment tribunals, but he also had a stack of civil files and, when I look back, it was reckless of me to put him into an office without proper support – given his lack of experience.

However, Donald was no shirker and when he came across a number of civil files which were in danger of falling foul of time barriers, he relied heavily and successfully on the efforts of our civil partner in Glasgow, the young Kenneth Mitchell. Kenneth spared no time and effort, and brought all Donald's civil files up to date. In any event, when still a partner with us, the seat of Garscadden became vacant and I have never stood in the way of anyone's political career. In fact, I have encouraged it. Donald won the seat.

Although Labour, Donald had been educated at Glasgow Academy, one of Glasgow's foremost private schools. His father was a doctor and he had inherited some paintings. He was therefore, if he put his mind to it, reasonably well off. But, of course, he didn't put his mind to any investments and he was off our payroll when he became a Member of Parliament. I still remember his gratitude when I paid over some money to him. Eventually, he retired as a partner of the firm and our paths crossed less frequently. But he was always a good and loyal friend, as I was to him. I put some of his financial affairs in the hands of a stockbroker friend.

At one time, when he became First Minister for Scotland, he became ill and had to undergo heart surgery to repair a leaking valve. Eventually he was sent home and confined to bed. It is not really in my nature to visit the sick, but our long friendship took over. I arranged for one of our staff to buy a lunch and took it with me to Donald's house. He ate in bed and never stopped talking (what was new?). He even recalled how we'd set up the Harper Thaw News Agency and he used to do reporting for that.

But, unhappily, I received a telephone call in October 2000 from Lewis Moonie, another Labour MP, to inform me that Donald had just died. He had returned to work after recuperating but, after only a couple of months, he sustained a fall as he left Bute House in Edinburgh and a brain haemorrhage later that day proved fatal. The world was a poorer place. Needless to say, his funeral/memorial service was fully attended and tributes flowed in. Glasgow University students lined University Avenue as his cortege went past. He had become a truly great and national figure, but I still remember him as 'the gannet', though with the greatest of affection.

I knew very well a man whom I thought should have been Prime Minister – Malcolm Rifkind. He was also a member of the Scottish Bar. My first real encounter with him was at Coatbridge when, by mistake, we had both been asked to speak to the local Conservative Association. In any event, we both turned up, so what else was there to do but for the Association to stage a debate? The subject chosen was capital punishment.

Malcolm was against it and I was ambivalent (the usual story, would say my detractors). It was Sir Roger de Coverley who said adroitly, 'There is much to be said on both sides.' In any event, Malcolm argued against and I argued for. Goodness knows what the result of the debate was, but capital punishment in these days was pretty popular.

I instructed Malcolm at the Bar and, indeed, he did his first major High Court case for two accused (which was most unusual in these days). The result I do not recall but Malcolm was a great, if not then experienced, performer.

He rose to the highest of offices, the number of which I suspect even he himself lost count. He was in charge of Scotland, at one point in charge of transport (he used to call it 'trains') and eventually reached the pinnacle of being Foreign Secretary in the mid-1990s.

When I was President of the International Bar Association I managed, via one of Malcolm's personal assistants, to arrange for him to open new IBA offices in London. This in itself was quite a coup and he was, as expected, immaculate in his opening speech.

He has been a companion a number of times, fishing in the Tay, even though the first time he came his assistant, Graham Carter, brought for him a trout net which was so small that I remarked it would barely hold our bait. I invited him fishing again recently but, unfortunately, Parliament was sitting and he still takes his duties seriously. I wrote to him saying that he ought to have been Prime Minister and he replied with his usual witticisms that he had no wish to be Prime Minister, but had a wish that he had been Prime Minister, or words to that effect. He would, in my humble opinion, have been outstanding.

Ian Duncan Smith was Leader of the Opposition in the early 2000s and should have become Prime Minister. Unhappily, whether it was because of style or substance, I know not, he was deposed by a Tory rebellion. Shortly after that, he was a guest of mine fishing on the Tay. A most charming and convivial man, but obviously the scars of his dethronement still remained. Nevertheless his wit continued. I remember placing him in the boat with Lewis Moonie and he then used a shooting term, remarking that was a right and a left, where you down two birds, one with each barrel of a double-barrelled shotgun.

He fell from grace by borrowing a spinning rod of mine. He tripped over the ground on his way back and broke the rod cleanly in two. Of course he offered to replace the rod, but I steadfastly refused. I think he acquitted himself quite well at salmon fishing and he was adamant that I should come with him to fish in the Test. But after that he was very busy and, perhaps understandably, I am still waiting. I did however receive a very gracious letter of thanks from him and his wife.

Interestingly enough he was the only one of my many acquaintances still to hold cabinet office up until this year. He resigned in March 2016 on the grounds that he could not accept proposed cuts in disability benefits or the austerity measures still being put forward by the government. A pity, as I understand that he was doing a very good job.

John Mackay became a very close friend of mine. He was an MP for Argyll. I remember once when he was fishing, he received a telephone call from Malcolm Rifkind asking him to become Under Secretary of State – a great honour – and a good evening we had celebrating.

But he was to lose his seat at the next election and eventually applied for a safe Conservative seat (at that time) of Ayr. On the way home from fishing we were listening to the radio when it was announced that he had not even made the final list for selection. An unhappy journey home. No one had bothered to tell him, apart from the BBC News. Such is politics – you need a thick skin to survive!

Nevertheless, he was transferred to the House of Lords. Normally House of Commons speakers do not shine in the House of Lords – the ambience and rhetoric is so different. For some reason John Mackay took to the House of Lords like a duck to water and became the star attraction. He was progressing so quickly that, having moved up the ladder, he was in line to become the equivalent of the Speaker. Unhappily, disaster struck. John Mackay's father had died at an early age of a heart attack. And so did John in 2001.

This was a tragedy for someone who was on the threshold of a new, exciting and glittering career. I was asked to deliver a memorial address at Glasgow Cathedral. I carefully prepared and memorised word-for-word my knowledge and appreciation of John. It must have been such a success that I was invited subsequently for a repeat performance in London at St Stephen's Church, opposite the House of Lords. Everybody but everybody was present, leaders of both parties included.

I recalled visiting him in the House of Lords (and I was careful to accentuate that I was a visitor only) and that, as I went through the corridors, John Mackay was regaled and patted on the back with a series of 'well done' comments after another bravura performance. John could, of course, have lapped it up all day, but it was too much for me. After all, I was a mate. I recall that I asked him to take me to the bar and give me a drink and tell me about the salmon which he lost on the previous week. Fishing is a great leveller!

I am vain enough to think that the speech went well, even if I did forget to bow to the priest or minister or whatever when I left the pulpit. Lord Strathclyde was able to usher me back to carry out the formality.

Michael Forsyth was one of the most interesting politicians whom I have ever met. He was cerebral, articulate and had an excess of confidence which is rarely met. He was an acolyte and a devotee of Thatcher and that admiration was clearly returned. Our paths crossed for good and bad in a number of ways. When I was chairman of the voluntary side, he was made president of the Conservative Party in Scotland – even though he was a sitting Member of Parliament. Despite my nomination for this plumb post by Malcolm Rifkind, he was appointed, much to the consternation of some of the anti-right-wingers in the party. I endeavoured to keep the peace and, since he was chairman, gave him my support.

Initially, he tried to dictate everything, including employees on the voluntary side, but was successfully, and somewhat bravely, resisted. I think at that time he was an Under-Secretary of State for Scotland and tried successfully to combine the two roles. I quarrelled with him at times but eventually, when I resigned from the chairmanship of the party, he endeavoured to make up. Indeed, since that time, I have been invited to join a number of fishing trips to Iceland. Where he did not always admire my left-wing Conservative politics, he did admire my ability to cast a fly in the waters.

When he was a minister within the Home Office, I arranged a meeting with him for my then clients, William Hill. They really retained me as a political consultant and admired me for my ability to fix meetings, including luncheons with ministers.

I recall Forsyth at his best. He responded to some of the pleas from the William Hill spokesman but at one time a civil servant beside him spoke out against a particular suggestion. Much to my surprise, Forsyth, in the presence of us all, turned on the hapless civil servant and upbraided him. My admiration for him notably increased.

Eventually, he lost his seat in Stirling and was quickly inflated to the House of Lords as Lord Forsyth of Drumlean in 1999 – still only in his mid-forties – but for some reason did not retain the unstinting admiration of the powers that be. I expected him to become Leader of the House of Lords, but that was not to be.

He succeeded Ian Lang as Secretary of State for Scotland at a time when my name had been put forward for a seat in the House of Lords. I was championed by Raymond Robertson, who always had enmity with Forsyth. I had always blamed Forsyth for stopping my entry, but I think I was proven wrong. But when asked his opinion, as he would be, as Secretary of State for Scotland, he referred the matter to the Lord Advocate, who apparently was against the idea of a Glaswegian former criminal lawyer securing entry to the House of Lords. It was so near and yet so far.

I was once able to do Michael Forsyth a great favour. One of his very close friends got into trouble with the police and faced prosecution. If I had any skills at all it would be dealing with potential prosecutions and I was able to avert the case, eventually sending my final plea to the procurator fiscal in charge. I am sure that Michael Forsyth did not agree with my letter but, lo and behold, it worked and justice was triumphant. He wanted to pay a fee but I resisted, against all my former principles of NFNP.

He had a glittering business career after he left Parliament, working for a merchant bank and other companies. As expected, he was intensely successful in his career. An interesting, competitive, able campaigner of right-wing causes.

Douglas Alexander was another of my fishing guests. He was the son of one of my closest friends at school and at university, also called Douglas Alexander, a Church of Scotland minister, recalled in an earlier chapter. He and his sister Wendy were both engaged in politics – Wendy in the Scottish Parliament and Douglas in Westminster. He rose to fame but very sadly lost at the 2015 general election when the SNP swept to power.

I recall advising him about apprenticeships when he was studying for the law, but clearly politics was in his blood. As was fishing. He once came up with his father and enjoyed a day's fishing, going home with a boot load of salmon. A very engaging character and extremely approachable.

Once during the fishing I saved him from a fate when he started to promise a person he had never met before that he would take him for lunch in the House of Commons. I knew he was too busy for such an offer and managed to shroud it with uncertainty. I hope he was grateful and, despite his politics, wish him well in his future career.

Michael Portillo was an interesting man. I did not like him at all at first. He was far too right-wing, but was clearly anxious for high office. I recall a Tory Party conference in England where, as a cabinet minister, he strayed from his brief. He used all his powers of oratory, which were extensive, even quoting from the film *Who Dares Wins*. He received rapturous applause from a gullible assembly of Tory faithful. I was one of the few, if not the only one, who did not clap. And newspaper reports proved me right. He received extremely bad press for his whole performance.

On another occasion he was in my house at election time, visiting a number of neighbours and friends whom I had assembled. He surprised me, not only with his pleasant manner, but also his vast knowledge of Scottish art – which impressed me all the more when he viewed my paintings. Apparently he had some Scottish relative who had left him some very fine art. I took to him.

I then followed and supported his progress to become Leader of the Party at the time of an election within the Conservative Party. I recall attending a morning meeting where he was regaled by the worst of the Party. He was questioned about Tory Party policy as only Conservatives can do. But he struck me as being remarkably calm and thoughtful. I jaloused that he already knew that he was not going to win the election. After that he became a formidable journalist and a very engaging and entertaining television presenter.

Lord Irvine of Lairg – Derry Irvine – is one of the most interesting and able men whom I have met over the years. He was a Glasgow graduate and an English barrister and a great friend of John Smith, although I did not really know him at the time. It is alleged that, being a brainbox, he actually wrote an essay for John Smith to secure him his class ticket. Whether that story is true or not I do not know, but it is certainly believable. He was a most successful barrister and graduated with distinction both at Glasgow and Cambridge.

I recall arranging for my son Robin to visit his Chambers in the hope that he would be influenced to join the English Bar. He was advised in no uncertain terms by Derry Irvine that he should go to Cambridge since all he held was a first-class honours from Strathclyde University – a 'Mickey Mouse degree' remarked Irvine, somewhat scathingly.

John Smith took me to visit him several times at his house and he was an avid Scottish art collector and, aided and abetted by his wife Alison, was very knowledgeable. If he was bidding at an auction through his agent, I would hastily withdraw, although I did buy a Fergusson which had been formerly owned by him, which I have since, unhappily, sold.

He came to my house on two or three occasions. I recall at a party he seized on the most excellent wine which I had bought and hidden away. John Mackay was there and foolishly tried to keep up with Derry Irvine's capacity for drink. If there was ever an impossibility, that was it.

On another occasion we had a dinner party at our London home. Francis Neate, senior partner of Slaughter and May's and a colleague of mine at the International Bar Association, was present and the conversation between two extremely opinionated and articulate successful men was a pleasure to behold. All the more so when fuelled by wine. Derry Irvine had scorned my first choice of a most excellent Spanish wine, saying that he did not drink wines unless from France. I reluctantly opened a bottle of wine that had been given to me by the managing director of Rothschild's after the coal privatisation. It was so delicious that, when placed in front of Derry Irvine, two or three others around the table had no chance.

Being a great friend of John Smith, he was also a friend of Tony Blair. In fact, Tony Blair, for a time, was a junior barrister and Derry knew him well. The story goes that at one time when he was visiting Downing Street when Blair was Prime Minister, Derry Irvine asked him to pour some wine, calling him 'my boy'. Again, whether this story is true or apocryphal I have no idea, but it does fit the man.

He is resourceful, ability oozing out of every pore, but, to his fault or credit, he is decidedly imperious. He rose to the top within the Labour Party as Lord Chancellor, but then he was suddenly and rather surprisingly replaced. However, by historical tradition, the Lord Chancellor's pension, no matter how long one holds the office, is among the best in the political landscape. It has been my pleasure still to meet Derry Irvine on occasions, dining at his favourite restaurant (for which he is ruthless in his choice).

Speaking of cerebral politicians, Lewis Moonie is a doctor,

although obviously doesn't believe in diets! I came across him because he joined our fishing fraternity and I have fished with him many times on the Tay. His only problem is, because of his weight, he requires to be in the boat most of the time. I always eschewed the boat but, as I got older, I must confess I do not relish wading in fast water, or indeed walking too far along the bank. But it keeps one fit.

Lewis Moonie would go to bed on an evening and finish the *Herald* crossword in about ten or fifteen minutes. He is an extremely intelligent and very pleasant man. He was a Member of Parliament for nearly twenty years, until 2005, and should have been promoted much earlier to ministerial ranks. Eventually he received the news (when we were fishing) that he had been given a ministerial appointment and much was the joy amongst his friends. He was in the Defence team, as junior minister, but eventually his boundaries changed, surrendering much of his Kirkcaldy constituency to the neighbouring constituency of Gordon Brown.

He was then 'promoted' to the House of Lords in 2005 but unhappily did not see Ministry again. He did, however, become involved in business and took to it like a duck to water being, as would be expected, successful.

George Younger was Secretary of State for Scotland and I think he was the person instrumental in securing for me the honour of a CBE – Commander of the British Empire. I came home one evening and opened the mail and here, to my surprise, was an official-looking letter in 1986, saying that I had been offered this honour. Would I accept? You bet! Many of my colleagues had received MBEs and OBEs, but CBE was second only to a Knighthood. Not being one to take risks, I jumped in the car and posted the acceptance at the post office that evening.

We were invited to Buckingham Palace to receive the

award and I was allowed to bring my wife and two other guests. Well, I had three children. What to do? I have only one daughter, Susan, and she exercised her 'rights' by saying that she intended to attend. The two brothers could spin a coin. I am not sure that they were particularly chuffed with this idea, each with a 50% chance of attending. Michael was at boarding school and I arranged for a coin to be spun – perhaps by the headmaster – and Robin won. Poor Michael.

In any event, all dressed up, we went to Buckingham Palace and Michael stood outside ready to greet us when we came out. It was a dramatic day. We were ejected from the palace late morning. I had been warned that I must arrange something at lunchtime, otherwise the day would fall flat. Unhappily my first choice of the House of Commons was not possible because it was in recess at the time. Accordingly, I arranged a luncheon at the Ritz, to which I invited Nicholas Fairbairn. A splendid day all round!

In any event, George Younger was a star performer and later became chairman of the Royal Bank of Scotland in 1992. He was still in Parliament at that time, but engaged heavily in bank duties. Margaret Thatcher used him as her campaign adviser when there was an election within the Conservative Party after a motion to depose her in 1990. Unhappily for her (and for George Younger) she lost that election. I miss George Younger and think of him fondly.

Jamie Lindsay was an exceptionally delightful companion, as was his wife Diana. We met his wife again when she was at a horse show with her children in Glasgow. Ursula and Diana shared a deep love for horses.

I made what was, in retrospect, a potentially serious mistake. I enthused about politics and said to Jamie that if he was ever offered a political appointment he should jump at it. The trouble was, I convinced him. There was a vacancy, an Under

Secretary of State for Scotland, held by a Member of the House of Lords. And there were not all that many candidates who were suitable. The Secretary of State for Scotland approached other parties and asked if there would be any objection if I was appointed in the House of Lords and immediately made Under Secretary.

But there was one last throw. They also approached Jamie Lindsay and he accepted. Nearly there, but yet again, not quite. In any event, Jamie Lindsay was a good Under Secretary of State for Scotland, although one of his claims to fame was that he was so polite that he insisted on opening his chauffeur's door rather than the reverse.

And then there was Struan Stevenson, a Member of Parliament for Europe. The Chairman of the Conservative Party, Raymond Robertson, had become unpopular with one or two others who exercised power and influence and they were trying to remove him. Such removal could only take place if the majority of the executive supported that. Malcolm Rifkind was acting as a champion and unofficial adviser to Raymond Robertson, and Raymond Robertson was confiding in me. Raymond was going to lose by one vote, according to the pundits, but there was an absentee member – Struan Stevenson – who was on holiday in Spain with no plans to return for the vote.

What to do? My regard for Raymond Robertson and dislike of the rebels was so high that I offered to pay for Stevenson's airfare to return. Malcolm Rifkind arranged that, stating that an anonymous donor of integrity would pay for his fare. Stevenson duly turned up, confounded the rebels and secured Raymond Robertson's position. My joy for Raymond was only shaken when I saw the amount of the airfare. It certainly was not a cheap package offer!

Russell Sanderson was chairman of the Conservative Party

in Scotland and later of England. An unusual occurrence. He was elevated to the House of Lords and was always a man held high in my esteem. I recall at one time my daughter (or rather her mother) wished to purchase a pony. This was owned by Russell Sanderson and I thought the price was too high. I remember stating that I would phone him and negotiate the price. I lowered the asking price and offered however many thousand guineas. In the old days all horses were sold in guineas, which, of course, is one pound one shilling. I think he was intrigued by the offer and accepted it. I went pale for a minute or two afterwards, thinking that I maybe had miscounted and that the offer I made him in guineas was in excess of the price he wanted in pounds. Fortunately my arithmetic had not let me down.

Tom Strathclyde was a very interesting man. He held a hereditary peerage, his father being a Member of Parliament in earlier days (much earlier) for Hillhead which, at that stage, returned a Conservative Member of Parliament. No longer – for many years. He is an engaging man and I developed a friendship with him, though that friendship did not translate into his helping me to be appointed to the House of Lords when Tony Blair was Prime Minister. I was deferred to a wealthy businessman (very wealthy), Lord Laidlaw, who had unmentionable troubles and has departed the UK.

Strathclyde was Leader of the House of Lords from 2010 to 2013 and looked ensconced to stay there for a further substantial time. Suddenly, however, he resigned, to further pursue a career in business. I do recall visiting him in his Leader's office, admiring the surroundings, and wishing him every success. In his own unique way, a delightful man and it was a pleasure to know him.

No chapter would be complete without mention of one of my favourites, Meta Ramsay, now Lady Ramsay (of Cartvale).

A delightful lady whom I have known, admired and respected since university days. President on numerous student bodies and engaged in international student affairs, she disappeared off the radar to the foreign office. Rumoured, but always denied, to have been a Scandinavian spook. She ended up in the Lords and did not obtain her proper elevation, although I think at one time she was a whip, albeit for the wrong party!

Over the last forty or fifty years, my political interests have brought me into close contact with many of the great figures of the time, from all parts of the political landscape. It has been, mostly, a pleasure to meet and know these men and women of influence and power and to know some small part of the work they were trying to do and the political machinations which went on so often behind the scenes. Perhaps in a very minor way I managed to exercise just a little influence for the good. Maybe just wishful thinking or a bad habit – or is it?

20

SCOTTISH COAL

In 1994 I moved from some forty years in the law to many years in mining. What a transition! The practice of mining is just as enjoyable, although a lot more nerve-wracking than the practice of the law. I used to quote that a director of a mining company needs balls of brass. And, of course, I was right.

But how on earth did I become involved in mining? When I was still in practice I recall a conversation on the banks of the River Tay with Colin Cornes – a man whom I used to admire seriously. He had many qualities and one of them was foresight. At that time there were plans by the government to privatise coal, and understandably so. Colin Cornes thought that we should make a bid for the Scottish end, as he averred (quite correctly) that Scotland was just full of coal.

So far, so good. The government's first plans, however, were disastrous for any Cornes-Harper schemes. I should explain that, despite his wealth, Colin Cornes could not make a bid of millions. The answer? Set up a consortium. This we planned to do, or rather *he* planned. We were due to start with a difficulty. The initial government plans were that the UK should be split, by area, into separate privatisations. That was good news. The bad news was that Scotland was to be lumped in with the north of England and much of the north of England, even after the aftermath of the unsuccessful miners' strike, was relatively difficult, if not impossible, to manage.

My first task, therefore, was to convince the government to redraw the boundaries. I approached Malcolm Rifkind and, although he was Secretary of State for Scotland at the time, he was able to point out to me that decisions on such matters lay with the Department of Trade. Who was in charge at that time? None other than Michael Heseltine.

Never being one to shirk my duty, I travelled up to Inverness where the Conservative Party Conference was being held. I made elaborate, if not somewhat devious, arrangements to meet with the great man himself. Heseltine agreed to spare ten minutes or so and joined me for a coffee. Without showing the inclinations to, or sympathy for, Scottish Nationalism, I argued that Scotland should be privatised separately, and I am happy to say that my plea did not fall on deaf ears. The territories were changed and Scotland was open for its coal-fields. It had one deep mine – at Longannet – and a number of surface mines – called 'open cast'.

So far, so good. But a consortium? Colin Cornes was in association with a major company in Birmingham. He invited the managing director for fishing – Malcolm Woods, a delightful companion. His only fault was to produce excellent bottles of Montrachet and allow the ghillies to drink and, as other ghillies appeared, the beautiful Montrachet was drunk like beer.

At that early stage in preparation it was appreciated that we would be flying a Scottish flag in terms of our bid. One of the other contenders would be a consortium put forward by some former management and unions and this consortium was advised by George Younger, who at that time was chairman of the Royal Bank of Scotland. Not being afraid to use past acquaintances, I recall visiting him in his palatial offices, and he said that he would try to arrange an amalgamation between our fledgling consortium and theirs. They needed some industrial muscle and we need grassroots support. The amalgamation was successfully arranged. But the major advance on our bid was the appearance of a partner of Cooper & Lybrand, Accountants (as it then was).

Our firm used them as auditors and I was able to secure an introduction to one of their partners in Edinburgh who dealt with commercial matters. His name was Nick Parker. And how lucky I was. He was guide, mentor, advisor and executive – all rolled into one. He threw himself into the idea of a bid with relish and a gusto which I have rarely seen elsewhere. We became friendly and I was happy to follow in his experienced footsteps. He introduced Murray Johnstone, a large financial firm, one of the principals of which I played rubber bridge with on occasions at the Western Club. That again was a success and Murray Johnstone was swept up in the euphoria that we could actually privatise Scottish Coal.

The pace increased. Colin Cornes produced two friends, John Savile and Bill Francis, who each were going to put in half a million pounds. Malcolm Edwards, a former senior director of the National Coal Board, was in charge of marketing. He had founded a coal company and came in with about 30%. There was also William Patterson of Waverley Mining, who had a percentage too. The consortium was large and at times unwieldy. We realised that we could now have the financial support. I went to my bank and arranged personal facilities for half a million pounds. I now regret this.

One, if not two, rooms in our legal office were taken over by coal. My partners were extremely forbearing, since we were on a no win, no fee basis, that is to say, if we didn't win the bid there would be no charge. If we did win then, of course, that was different. We even employed a temporary chief executive to help mastermind the operation – businessman Brian MacDonald.

A bid was assembled with reams of accompanying paper, but what we needed was a chairman of note. Fortunately, joining us occasionally in fishing was a chief executive of Scottish Power, at that time one of Scotland's most successful companies. He was due to retire and in great secrecy agreed that on his retirement he would take over as chairman – that is if we were successful. Such a move had to be conducted in the greatest of secrecy and I put his name in a sealed envelope, only to be opened by the government and their advisors and to be kept confidential. This worked.

In any event, the bid, which was extremely professionally prepared, was duly lodged. Colin Cornes, for obvious reasons, had very little to do with the preparation of the legalities. The only time he endeavoured to make his voice heard was just before the bid was due to make up our mind how much we should offer. There was a meeting of those involved, including Nick Parker, on whose advice I was ready to rely. The discussion was wide. Colin Cornes wanted to offer a lot more than any of the rest of us.

This was a difficult decision. The tender was to be submitted and we were against some opposition. On the other hand, there were many problems within the business. The assets were solid, but we would be taking over liabilities, such as claims by other parties. In any event, in an effort to reach a conclusion, I asked all present at the meeting to write on a bit of paper their name and their suggested tender offer. Perhaps it was no surprise that

Colin Cornes was well in excess of the others.

We did fix an amount, in the tens of millions. The offer was successful to the extent that we were in a short leet of one – although the government, which was masterminding the deal, was free at any time to call in one of the others who had made a tender. There was a long way to go.

We were called to a meeting at Rothschilds. I still remember the managing director in charge of what even for them was a fairly large transaction. He started off rather dictatorially by saying that he was there to advise what we were required to do and he would not be answering questions. Sir William Francis, who was part of our small delegation and not short of boardroom experience and cunning, interrupted the speaker by asking a question about timing; a question which he had to answer. Supplicants one – Rothschilds nil.

We had devised a name – Mining Scotland Limited – and set about our task. This was significant. Nick Parker brought in an assistant, Paul Brewer, who shone and eventually became a partner in Coopers & Lybrand. On the legal side we had Len Freedman and later seconded a London lawyer with some experience to stay in Glasgow and join the team. The meetings with Rothschilds, all held at Rothschilds, were extensive and detailed. Any draft agreements they produced we tried to amend. We also tried to receive indemnities from the claims against the then National Coal Board in Scotland.

We visited the deep mine. I still remember Nick Parker came down and sat on a small train. These trains were called man-riders and sailed into the depths of the mine, depositing miners at various stages. On reaching the equivalent of a face, the man-riders were slowed down, but not stopped, and everybody had to tumble out as best they could. But not Nick Parker. He must have left his descent until the last minute and, lo and behold, he ended up against a mine wall, I suspect rather like Corky the Cat. He was injured and I think he still suffers a little from that. He refused, however, to intimate a claim and, indeed, all credit to him.

We finally reached agreement with the government and Rothschilds and found the appropriate money, after many last-minute difficulties, and became the owner of Scottish Coal with considerable negotiations about our ability to use the word 'Scottish', which we made a condition of the deal. The chap in Rothschilds in charge of the negotiations with us eventually became its managing director. I was lucky; he raided the Rothschilds' cellar and gave me a most excellent bottle of wine, the fate of which I outlined earlier.

We had as managing director, a former British Coal senior employee. He stamped his authority on the proceedings by refusing a suggestion by Bill Francis that we should split up into two companies – a deep mine and open cast. This had been a truly excellent suggestion, but unfortunately denied.

A lot of this had to do with the morale of the deep mine employees. And so we continued. I was made deputy chairman (somewhat to my surprise, but delight). Preston, the former Scottish Power executive, conducted himself well as chairman, but he took on too many commitments and was unable to give too much attention to the job. Nevertheless, he was a steadying influence for which I was extremely grateful.

One trauma took place fairly early on when Colin Cornes decided to take matters of planning permission into his own hands and started dealing directly with the council responsible for such matters. He must have thought at the time that this was the best way to proceed but it didn't go quite as he'd planned. In fact, as I recall, all hell broke loose. The position was saved when I was able to bring in the right consultant who really knew how the system worked and was able to sort out the planning permission we needed to mine coal.

But after that trauma there were more traumas to come. One of our minority shareholders, a company owned by Malcolm Edwards, went into liquidation. Liquidators appointed a director (as was a company's right to do), a certain Ivor Kelly who was one of the most interesting men I have ever met. He had a fierce intellect, was very articulate and was a man much used to getting his own way.

The good news was that he proposed, and helped to engineer, the separation of the deep mine and open cast businesses. The bad news was that doing this was not universally popular and those opposed dug their heels in. In every successful company, there requires, in my opinion, to be harmony, if not outright peace.

One of the changes which Ivor Kelly wanted to implement was the resignation of our chairman, who had become horrendously busy with other matters. To my surprise and astonishment it was proposed by the Board that I should become the chairman. Chairman of a very large mining company – as a former Glasgow solicitor!

Naturally, never being fearful and always responsive to challenges, I accepted this job and, on the whole, enjoyed it. I kept mostly in touch with the chief executive – at that time Peter Lawwell – who is now the chief executive of Celtic Football Club. In my view he was a star and battled through many, many problems.

We had been inundated with claims and, indeed, the price we paid reflected to some extent the value of these claims. These were usually from open cast contractors and started in the days of British Coal. What better task for a lawyer? I took the responsibility of fighting each and every claim. If my recollection is correct, we had an unbelievable success rate – apart from one where Colin Cornes decided to take the matter into his own hands. He went to see the principal of the claimant, coming back with what he thought was a good settlement.

I was livid. It was not the way we were doing things at that time. He had been accompanied by someone from Scottish Coal's claims team, a team that, it seemed to me, advocated settlement of claims more often that not. In this case, as I recall, a settlement agreement was signed there and then and there was no prospect of extricating the company from it. It was a done deal but not the sort of deal we should have been doing. To be fair, Colin Cornes did many positive things for the company but I think that sometimes, as in this case, he got it wrong. After all these years I can still feel how angry I was that day.

We still had one major claim to go, but we were saved from the effects of this by the good fortune that the claimant ceased trading. Colin Cornes was able to come to an arrangement with the liquidator of our shareholding company and bought Malcolm Edward's shares. The balance of the company then changed dramatically.

The good news, as far as my sanity was concerned, was that Ivor Kelly departed. The problem for me, however, was that Colin Cornes then became a majority shareholder with considerably increased power.

One of my earliest run-ins with Ivor Kelly was when we were making a complicated arrangement with Scottish Power and another Scottish energy company. There were advantages which were useful to both parties and it was a complicated legal agreement. It was agreed that this would be signed one Sunday in our offices, but there was still some negotiation to be done. So we arranged for typists come into the office and many discussions (some heated) took place.

We were nearly at peace after some hours, but there was no settling some of Ivor Kelly's concerns, which we adduced were minor. Nevertheless, he exercised severe influence in the negotiations and we were in danger of lasting not only a day but a week – or even more. It was important for us that the deal was concluded, but the position became fraught and some of those from the other companies indicated that their directors, who were there to sign the deal, would shortly be going home.

What to do? An unwilling Scottish Coal representative and customers were about to go home. I still remember taking the bull by the horns and calling a meeting with the parties. Ivor Kelly was in another room and didn't come to the meeting. He was still wrestling with the draft of a draft of a draft. The meeting concluded in agreement and I obtained the signatures of all those concerned and appended my own as Peter Lawwell appended his. Everybody was in the process of going home when Ivor Kelly came through and I had to tell him he was too late. The deal was signed! I don't suppose he has ever forgiven me – but needs must.

However, he was no more. Colin Cornes was everywhere. But there was another problem – an insurmountable problem. A horrific problem.

The deep mine, which was the last deep mine in Scotland, had been struggling but was still producing coal. Whenever a fault was hit, a tunnel would have to be directed round the fault or in a different direction altogether. At that time we were underneath the Forth, or nearly underneath it. When we opened a new area I had arranged for Donald Dewar, then Secretary of State for Scotland, to come and conduct the grand opening. This impressed all concerned and I still recall him being fitted out in a miner's kit and emerging from the opening with a coal-stained face.

Naturally, the press were delighted. I recall him holding a piece of coal that had been delivered to him by a miner and smiling as he flourished it. I noticed that his arms were beginning to ache. A large piece of coal is relatively light. He had been given a piece of stone coloured like a piece of coal. Blushes all round. I suspect when coal was delivered to Scottish Power that there were many other pieces of stone in it, but it seemed to do the power station no harm.

But, tragedy was to befall us. I remember when I was in London receiving a phone call that the mine was flooded. Fortunately, nobody had been working in the area of the flooding but the water rose and rose. Apparently there was an adjoining mine which earlier had been flooded and, for some reason, water got into our mine. The good news was that there were no casualties. The bad news was that our mine became inoperable. A great deal of equipment was irretrievably lost and the last of the Scottish deep mines closed.

Needless to say there was great trauma, press and publicity with Members of Parliament involved. We required to hold a press conference at which everyone, including the local MP, expressed regret. I had prepared a very lengthy speech about all the work we had put into the deep mine, but Colin Cornes wisely advised me to cut it down. This I did.

The press conference could have been quite ugly, with the persistent questioning. Fortunately, at that time a liquidator had been appointed and it became known to the press that he was making his way to the deep mine at that minute. The journalists, who were ready to pursue me with questions, vanished like the snow off a dyke and this, I must confess, was a great relief to me. Ivor Kelly was decent enough to phone with his commiserations. He had spent a lot of time in the management of the deep mine and he had the ties. Pannell Kerr Forster were appointed liquidators.

We continued with the open cast with good days and bad days. I remember Peter Lawwell leaving to join Celtic

Football Club in 2003, and Colin Cornes sent a team of his own in – including his son Sam and an energetic and wise man called Brian Staples, who himself had had an interesting, and I suspect lucrative, business career. I must confess I did not agree with all the moves Colin Cornes made, but he was now the majority shareholder and the equivalent, therefore, of the owner.

We had our independent board members and I remember one objecting that Colin Cornes was using the company as a private fiefdom. He had of course no evidence of that but at one time I received a panicky phone call from his finance director in Birmingham to say that investigations were taking place into an allegation that company equipment was being misused. It seems strange now, but my recollection is that Colin was supposed to have had some piece of equipment or other in his garden! I told them to immediately make sure that was not the case and report back to confirm.

All the traumas of the investigation took place and, fortunately, the investigators produced a report clearing Colin. I had liaised with the investigation to make sure all would be well but I don't think Colin ever thanked me. In any event, he and I were becoming more distant, although fishing each year together. When the deep mine went under (literally) my salary went down without consultation. He continued to run a fiefdom and I continued to chair the board meetings leaving the experts (as I always do) plenty of room.

I had not heard from Colin Cornes for a week or two and, after chairing a board meeting, I was met at the Scottish Coal headquarters and had a meeting with a slightly embarrassed Brian Staples and, I am sure, an equally embarrassed Sam Cornes. Sam was the son whom I had befriended when he was a young lad. Well, Brian Staples produced the bombshell. I was being told to resign. Well I could not recall ever having been sacked before, but here I was – it is fair to say – gobsmacked! Not a murmur from Colin Cornes. Not a phone call. Sacking by a proxy. Embarrassing? You bet.

There was to be no notice and no compensation. Brian Staples said that since he was in charge of the administration of Scottish Coal at that time he would ensure that I would be paid for some months, unknown to Colin. I thanked him for his kindness but I did not want him to get into trouble over me and refused the offer.

Well, I did accept that I was being sacked. Rod McKenzie advised me that I should just have refused to resign and sat it out. I must confess that, while that was sensible legal advice, it's hardly my style. I did consult lawyers, however, and intimated a claim against Scottish Coal for lack of notice. Prior to that I had got something out of my system by arranging to meet Colin Cornes – travelling down to Birmingham where he agreed to have a lunch. He told me that his wife had advised him against attending the lunch. Well, when we met, I did not miss him. All to no avail, except that at the end of lunch he hugged me. Would you 'Adam and Eve' it?

During lunch I got him to disclose why he sacked me, and one of his reasons was that there was a Labour government and I was well known for being a Conservative. It was a bit silly since my contacts with the Labour Party were just as great if not greater than with the Conservative Party.

I took notes of this meeting to establish that in fact I had been sacked. He did raise his hand in some sort of apology that he had not undertaken the act himself and that he had sent another man and his son. Apparently this is not unusual conduct for him. He later disclosed to a member of a fishing party that he had parted company with me because I was 'too much a lawyer'. I treated this as a great compliment.

I consulted a lawyer who intimated a claim. I thought I

might as well try and obtain a few months' salary – or indeed a year's. The lawyer was met with the reply that I had voluntarily resigned. I did not think this was a fair or reasonable response. I was not being greedy. I was merely extremely upset and annoyed. And understandably so.

At this point our dealings got considerably more complex. They were clearly intent on sticking to their position and I was equally determined to make my case. However, it was made clear to me that if I pursued my case the consequences for certain people could be dire, personally and financially, and it would be, in effect, my responsibility. Clearly the company position was remaining rock solid and seemed totally inflexible. A dilemma was presented to me. Do I pursue my claim which could have a drastic effect on people I knew and had worked with or walk away? It was not a situation to be taken lightly but I knew what I had to do, however unpalatable.

It was against all my instincts and wishes, but sometimes one has to recognise when one is not in control. I have no means of knowing what the consequences would have been had I pursued my claim but it simply was not worth the risk. I decided to phone Colin and merely said, without raising my voice, 'You've won.' I think he agreed somewhat reluctantly to one or two months' salary. You win some, you lose some. When one is not in a powerful position, surrender is the only way out.

But what about Scottish Coal? When I was chairman we were looking closely at a flotation and had instructed brokers. Unhappily, Colin Cornes did not fancy selling out, or even retaining shares in a public company and the idea, much to my displeasure, came to nothing.

But about two years ago, after I left, the idea resurfaced and considerable work was carried out to ensure a flotation. Nick Parker was brought in as a chairman of the company and the way looked good. My half million shares could have been worth some three or four million pounds. As happens in flotations, however, the prospective price fluctuated and, when they fluctuated slightly downwards, Colin Cornes, for some reason best known to himself, perhaps acting on bad advice from doubtful sources, suddenly and without warning withdrew the flotation – and what looked a more than helpful bonanza vanished into coal dust.

Unhappily, the company did not prosper as forecast. Nick Parker was removed from the Board and various changes took place. One chairman who was appointed and who had brought us experience, unhappily died. His brother, who was an Edinburgh lawyer, took over, with, of course, unfortunate results for Harper Macleod, who had been doing most of the legal work. You win some, you lose some.

Through no fault of anyone's, the price of coal had plummeted and quite a number of coal companies within the UK are in serious distress. And now? Scottish Coal is no more – sunk – liquidated. Half a million pounds? Down the drain. And Colin Cornes? Ursula was always charmed by him and he was in many ways a giant and a gem of a man, greatly admired, and my many disagreements do not diminish my regard, bordering on affection.

But, in my view, it was more than unfortunate that Colin ended up as the majority shareholder. Had things been handled differently, there could have been a very much better outcome. That said, it was a rewarding experience in so many ways other than financial and fascinating to be involved in something so different to the law.

21

STILL WORKING IN
A COAL MINE

My experience in coal mining took me into two other mining ventures. The first was Admiralty Resources, a stock market listed company in Melbourne whose main activity relates to iron ore in Chile. The history of the company is complex but, at that time, one of the prime movers met me in London when I was introducing him to merchant bankers. In the course of this venture (engineered by my son Robin) and after I got to know him quite well, he offered me the chairmanship of Admiralty Resources, a public company.

I was never one to refuse an interesting offer. The salary he offered was almost mind-boggling – but the salary which was eventually settled was about a half of what had originally been offered and had tempted me to chair an Australian company, even though living at that time in London.

The managing director at that time was Philip Thomas – a

bull of a man and expert in most trades, including geology and stockbroking. But whatever else, the mining did not prosper and eventually we had to sell one of the assets. Philip Thomas became connected with the buyer in some strange way and the shareholders were, understandably, not at all pleased. In any event, Philip Thomas resigned so that he could associate himself with the company buying the asset and we were left without a managing director.

Another Board director, John Anderson, was brought in as chief executive at the recommendation of others on the Board. Now a chairman's duty is to support a managing director and I endeavoured so to do. We had a further managing director in Chile, a former senior officer of the Navy, but between them the company failed to prosper and sometimes was in difficult straits.

We needed a new member or two on the Board. John Anderson failed to put forward an acceptable name. The secretary, Steven Prior, put forward a name, Mike Perry, who was a responsible accountant – formerly a partner in one of the big four. By that time I was uneasy about John Anderson. He seemed rarely to attend the main office (Steven Prior's office) in which a room had been set aside for him. He lived a distance away. Indeed, when I was appointed I expressed my worry that he would be able to travel – all the more so since he had a dog to look after. The sort of thing a chairman must know! In any event, my relationship with him and our Chilean man did not progress well and I forecast potential disaster for the company.

As it happens, we were having an Annual General Meeting and when in Melbourne I stay at a club. On an evening (or two) before the Annual General Meeting I had dined alone at the club, having partaken of a couple of glasses of wine. After dinner I wanted to smoke a cigar and walked out of the club on to a main street which had a small thoroughfare. I woke up a week later in hospital remembering nothing; not even a visit from my son from Sydney, who I apparently could not recognise. I had been in a coma.

Well, what happened? I had been walking along a side street and fell. It was later thought that I had fallen over an outside chair. In any event, for some reason, I landed on my back and fractured my skull. Naturally the Annual General Meeting had to proceed without me (it is the only one I have missed in something like ten years). I was moved eventually from one hospital to another where I gradually recovered.

Ursula flew from London to Melbourne and stayed at the club, which made her very welcome. She spent day after day at my bedside as I slowly recovered. I was given all sorts of treatment and tests to ascertain whether there was any permanent damage. I have since been told that a few people, having had an equivalent fracture, died immediately. Perhaps the pavements in Melbourne were not as tough as some other pavements. I suspect it was my tough Scottish nut that saved me from death.

The hospital would have liked to keep me in for longer but I cajoled and made myself enough of a nuisance for them to release me, provided I would receive treatment when I got back to London. This I did and went through all sorts of medical contortions, speech therapy, mental tests and the like.

Fortunately, I survived, though there was an interesting sting in the tale. My medical bills in Melbourne and London were *ginormous!* And more. Nevertheless, I was insured and submitted a claim. This claim was refused and I was nonplussed.

Eventually, it turned out that the claim was refused because the accident was caused by alcohol. Now David, my son-in-law, thought that that was an improper reason and that I should fight. I did not fall down because I was drunk. I know when I am drunk and when I am not. I think I could safely count on the fingers of one hand or less the number of times I have been drunk – and I knew that night I was certainly not drunk. But I jaloused that there must be some reasoning behind the insurance company's decision. Fractured skull or not, I was sensible enough to telephone the first hospital which had taken me in and spoke to a very pleasant lady doctor who remembered me well. She agreed she would check the hospital records and I agreed to telephone her back.

She was able to tell me what my blood alcohol level was. Now I had done a series of drunk driving cases when I was young and I knew about blood alcohol levels. When she gave me the figure I realised I was not 'drunk'. In fact, on that level, I would have been fit to drive in the United Kingdom. But she was able to enlighten me. Australian drink driving laws are different and the alcohol level required to convict a person of drink driving was much lower than the UK. I had no quarrel (and indeed applaud that) but I knew that I had enough to challenge the insurance company in no uncertain terms. I obtained written notification of my level and David came to the rescue and the insurance company retracted its original decision. Some victories, however relatively minor, do give comfort.

At the time of my accident John Anderson appeared very sympathetic and helpful, but I think he knew that my opinion of him was low. In any event, the company received a letter from his solicitors asking that, because of my accident, I should resign as chairman. Would you believe it? I could not – but of course I had to take it somewhat seriously. I did not resign.

John Anderson continued on his merry way for a while, but I could feel that my views on him were getting considerable sympathy from the Board members. Eventually, and I take great pride in this, we agreed to appoint Steven Prior. He was the secretary of the company and had founded an excellent accountancy firm. He had been associated with Admiralty Resources for longer than I had and knew the ins and outs and the ups and downs. He took to the job like a duck to water and I kept up a very close relationship with him as he settled into the job and steered the company in the right direction.

A number of Chinese firms then took an interest in the company and we invited two of their directors (one living in Sydney) to be a director of the firm. They have a great knowledge of iron ore and are extremely helpful, albeit painstakingly detailed.

Basically, I am a company structure man looking at overall capital, overall finance and, of course, share price. One of the penalties (or perhaps pleasures) of being chairman of a public company is that the share price is important – although not to my mind the be all and end all. The duties of company directors are to ensure the company's stability, leading to profitability. The share price, while important, is not necessarily the criterion of success. Share prices are very temporary, but I sometimes feel I am in the minority with that particular view. Our duty is to the company and, therefore, to the shareholders for the long term.

So far, so good, but suddenly another Chinese person entered the scene, acquiring some 5% of the shares and, lo and behold, called for the removal of the chairman of the company (that is me) and the managing director (Steven Prior). I made a deal (what's new?). I would resign if Prior stayed. That was accepted.

Then I was approached by a relatively young man – Aaron Thomas, an Australian, who was at that time based in London. He was the son of Philip Thomas and had briefly worked in the Admiralty office. He is a very interesting and energetic man, although I had preached unsuccessfully to him on many occasions that delegation is the keynote to success, with supervision of course.

In any event, Oakmont was a company developing iron ore mining in Brazil. Fortunately, there was no conflict with Admiralty, which was iron ore mining in Chile. I was asked to become the chairman briefly and then, shortly after that, was told that another chairman had been appointed. Then I was again asked to be chairman and, a week or two after that, another chairman was appointed. In out, in out. And finally out, out and out.

Fortunately, I did not overly concern myself with this ritual dance and I recognised that the chairman who was eventually appointed, Gordon Todd, had first-hand experience of mining all his life and had been extremely successful. There is no way that somebody of my experience in mining could start, hope or expect to compete.

I warned Aaron Thomas that I would be staying in Australia but he did not seem to worry about that and, accordingly, I am flown back to London every quarter to attend Board meetings (that is if they are called!) The idea was that Oakmont would get reasonably advanced in its exploratory work in Brazil and then float as a public company. This idea appealed to me.

Oakmont is run entirely differently from Admiralty, which bases its work on sub-contracting. Oakmont seems to have more staff. It certainly has an impressive Board and there are four non-executives. The bit that was not impressive was that we were not paid!

While one can stand this for so long and, however enjoyable the activities of Aaron Thomas were, at the last Board meeting I stuck to my guns that payment should be made. I did not raise the matter earlier because the company simply did not have the funds. Aaron Thomas is, however, very adept at raising the funds from other sources and I reckoned that it was time for us to share in the good news.

It is too early to make a positive forecast about the company. I have backed it because of my regard for Aaron Thomas, but will it be an outstanding success or a flop? Obviously I hope the former, and I am reasonably confident. It is a mistake to have one's name associated with a flop – corporate life-threatening. But, of course, yet again – time will tell.

Now here is the irony of it all. I have heard nothing for years. I do not know if the company is still alive. I do not know if Aaron is still alive. He probably thinks I am dead. I do not know if they will ever pay me any money. Uncertainty is only outbid by total ignorance.

22

AFRICA

This is a story of two parts. The first ended in March 2003. The second will not end for perhaps some forty years. The heroine of the story (or could she be the villain?) is Susan Harper, my daughter. The focus of the story lies in Susan and her husband's random choice of a visit to Africa for their honeymoon. This choice had a devastating effect on Susan, which, in turn, had an equally devastating effect on Susan's husband and parents; and this is where the story really begins.

Susan was smitten by Africa; completely captivated. It does happen. It is said that Africa is the home and origin of man. There may be something in the air which welcomes some mortals back and something in the ambience which persuades them not to leave, whether it's the sheer beauty of the landscape, the brilliant nights, the raw energy of the animals, nature 'red in tooth and claw' we shall never know, nor ever need to know.

Suffice it to say that Susan was determined that she should eventually make Africa her part home and was equally determined that she should create a safari lodge set in a remote part of that continent. And what is just as extraordinary is that David, her husband, while not sharing the same passion, was happy to go along with her plans.

Now enter the second heroine/villain of the story – Ursula. She brought up three children in Scotland while looking after a husband and a menagerie of animals. Ursula is besotted with animals and a conservationist in the extreme. She once came out on a pheasant shoot and disappeared after the first shot – to drive the pheasants away from the guns. No spider or fly can be killed inside or outside the house. A mouse in the house is as liable to be entertained as exterminated. In its heyday, the Harper family had five horses, two dogs, seven cats, three parrots and a hamster. I used to claim that I ranked in the Harper household slightly below the hamster.

And now the coincidence. In the same year that Susan was honeymooning in South Africa, I foolishly delegated responsibility for the family holiday to Ursula, who booked up two weeks in Africa in diverse locations. She came back as smitten as her daughter, vowing to return to Africa again and again and again.

What could David and I do against two such determined women joined in a common purpose to purchase land in Africa? Susan and Ursula conspired, exemplifying the phrase, 'Real leaders are ordinary people with extraordinary determination.'

'Let's set up a company,' suggested Susan. Her idea was simple; namely, to rewrite company law textbooks and issue myself with shares which were non-voting, non-transferable, non-dividend bearing and non-convertible.

'Sounds pretty much like a gift to me,' I grumbled.

And so the quest began. Ursula and Susan determined to find somewhere quickly while David and I joined steadfastly together to delay the inevitable for as long as possible.

And so the family travelled to Africa one winter to look at propositions set up by Susan over the summer; not just in South Africa, but in Botswana, Zambia and a host of other places too numerous to recall. And some of the propositions even got to draft contract stage, but good luck favoured the men and there was always something wrong, either with the titles or the lodge or the personnel or the deal.

I started to read more and more about malaria and how many people were killed by it each year. Every time I was bitten by a mosquito I imagined cerebral malaria and was not pleased. Therefore, with the confidence of a coward, I said that the girls could buy any place they wanted in Africa, subject to the finance being available, but if it was located in an area where malaria was present, I, for one, would not be visiting it. Well, that caused a bit of consternation in the family and, for once in my life, I was afforded some attention.

David demanded that we must be confident about manage-ment and find the best manager in Africa; someone with bush experience. Well that was agreed and every time we went on safari, separately or together, each and every ranger was scrutinised as a possible manager. Many safaris were made. Indeed, Susan and her mother went on a walking safari with the legendary Lloyd Wilmot where Susan, quite improperly, went out of the vehicle to 'play' with the lions.

As site after site was inspected, site after site was rejected, much to the delight of the men and the frustration of the women. Perhaps the search might go on for a decade or two and, by that time, Susan would have continued work and saved enough money to allow her unwilling father to beat a hasty retreat to his fishing and pension. But suddenly the world was to change: a wonderful site became available. It met all the criteria – and more. Introduced by an indefatigable and companionable entre-preneur, William Stephens, a farm of 2,000 hectares incorporated into the Madikwe game reserve in South Africa, near the border with Botswana, was inspected.

First of all, it was malaria-free, so I could not complain and could visit it in safety. Secondly, it housed the 'Big Five' – lion, elephant, leopard, buffalo and rhino – in abundance. Ursula and Susan inspected. David was dragged over and serious negotiations took place. I could not find any method of sabotaging the deal, nor indeed, when I saw the place, did I want to. It was ideal.

There was a river, alongside which a lodge could be built. It was private land right in the middle of a well-managed, well-structured, extremely large reserve. But there was one criterion still missing: management was paramount, and while Ursula and Susan were Africa and animal fanatics, running a business was different.

The story then took another turning: fortune shone on Susan and Ursula because there entered into the scene the hero of the story – big, rangy, unforgettable, blond Garth Kew. Garth was the answer to everyone's dreams. He had worked in Madikwe for a number of years as tracker, ranger and manager and had already supervised the construction and start-up phase for another lodge in the area. Garth was ideal.

What a find! Contact was soon made with him and Garth became part of the family, displaying a patience and tolerance beyond belief, dealing with the female fanaticism and the male cynicism with equal aplomb. Contracts were soon exchanged and the money was paid.

The Harper family had secured a vast tract of exclusive and private land with a beautiful farmhouse, traversing rights over Madikwe Game Reserve and little else; except for a young lady with extraordinary determination aided and abetted, psychologically by her mother, and practically by Garth, the new managing director.

This was a real excuse for Susan and Ursula to visit Africa regularly. An award-winning international architect called Bruce Stafford was found (nothing but the best of course!), plans were submitted, planning permission was requested, environmental impact assessments were undertaken, swimming pools, gymnasiums, air conditioning, central heating, open fires, views of the river, luxurious staff accommodation – you name it – Susan and Garth provided it.

Now the original idea, well to the menfolk, was that the area was so big we could sell off parts of the land for others to build corporate lodges, thus paying for the construction of our lodge. But there was a change to that cunning plan. Would it not be better, argued the women, if the farm (inappropriately at that time called Krokodildrift) was exclusive?

'We should be able to show our guests round without crowds,' argued Susan. 'Businesses should have a unique selling point. Our unique selling point surely is exclusivity?'

And so no land was sold and no corporate lodges were built. But what about the name? I liked the name Krokodildrift, but perhaps there were no crocs in the river. 'Anyway, who really loves crocodiles?' asked Susan.

The most important feature of Krokodildrift and Madikwe itself was that of the wild dogs, rare in the rest of the world but plentiful in Madikwe. Therefore what about the name 'Wild Dogs'? Ugh. Wild dog in Tswana (the local language) was 'makanyane' and, after interminable debate, full consultation and in the greatest spirit of democracy, Susan determined that the name of the lodge should be Makanyane.

And so the first part of the story of Krokodildrift is nearly complete. And is the story going to end happily? We hope so. It's a marvellous story of determination and provides for the family a united purpose. And if we want an omen? A crocodile was recently spied in the river at Krokodildrift – sorry

Makanyane – for the first time in years. Are the African gods telling us something?'

Since Makanyane opened in 2003, it has been hugely successful. It has far exceeded our expectations in every aspect. We have had the families of two US presidents staying there and a number of celebrities. The reviews on TripAdvisor have been fantastic and the lodge has generated very positive feedback from a number of international publications. Perhaps best know for its honeymoons it has been popular with a range of people celebrating milestone celebrations. We had the wonderful Peter Alexander (the pyjama king) celebrate a significant birthday at Makanyane a couple of years ago and he has since revisited. Perhaps the most wonderful aspect of Makanyane is the fact that we have many people coming and discovering Africa here and then revisiting again and again. When you talk to people staying for the first time, you realise they are blown away by the experience.

Garth is still very much in charge, as is Dylan our head ranger who has been with us since the opening. The marketing of the lodge is now carried out by Sanctuary Retreats and we very much enjoy being part of this wonderful portfolio of luxury safari lodges.

I visit the lodge at least once a year with Ursula, Susan and David and their family and friends and we always have the most magical time. Ursula and Susan's love of the bush increases the more time they spend there. Ursula, Susan and her family visit at least twice a year and all her children have grown up with a love, and respect, for the bush and a passion for wildlife. It would not surprise me to see some if not all of her children spend a significant amount of time in Africa at some point in their lives.

23

ACCIDENTS WILL HAPPEN

I have had some scary moments staring at possible asphyxiation in the mirror. One time in the late 1990s, at home in Glasgow, a piece of meat lodged in the back of my throat, preventing me from breathing. I was obviously in distress and could not clear the air passageway.

Ursula took fright and phoned my brother, Murray. I looked in the mirror unable to breathe. Fortunately, the piece dislodged and I recovered. But that was only the beginning. My brother told me about the Heimlich manoeuvre, whereby, if a person is choking another person stands behind him and presses below the rib cage at the stomach, very hard; this expels air and often removes the offending article.

Another time I was at a very expensive restaurant welcoming two or three new partners and, during the course of the meal, because I was talking and eating – an extremely bad habit – I did not swallow a piece of meat properly and began to get breathless and was unable to breathe. When it stuck in my throat, I retreated to the gents. The obstruction would not dislodge.

I called in a Spanish waiter and told him what he had to do. He saw that I was obviously in distress but mistook my signals and thought I wanted to press him on the chest. Eventually I was able to communicate and when he stood behind me, he pressed me and my food dislodged. After recovering for a few minutes, I returned to the table pretending that nothing was wrong.

The other time when that serious event happened I was staying at the Tayside Hotel near Perth. Again, talking and eating meat, I felt it lodge. Unable to breathe, I retreated to the gents and tried in vain to budge it. I must have been without breath for a few minutes and one of my fishing friends, a senior policeman, came through to find out if I was all right. He immediately saw what was wrong and he knew the Heimlich manoeuvre. He was a big strong lad and pressed so hard that my food was immediately dislodged. The slight trouble was that he pressed so hard that he fractured one of my ribs! However, I was still alive, thankfully.

Thus frightened, I consulted medical opinion, and it was diagnosed that I had a pharyngeal pouch. This meant that in my windpipe there was an unnatural pouch and I required surgery. Surgeons were not used to removing pharyngal pouches and I was placed in the hands of a specialist – an ear, nose and throat surgeon whom I suspect had never before conducted this operation. I toddled into hospital, requiring my beard to be shaved off before I entered. The operation and aftermath were bordering on horrific and, when I recovered, I was told that I would be right as rain. Unhappily, my symptoms persisted and, after another X-ray, it was discovered that the surgeon had gone to the wrong side of the windpipe and my pharyngeal pouch was still there.

There was nothing for it but a repeat operation; again horrific. I recovered but still, some twenty years later, I remain very wary of eating meat. Certainly, I never talk when I am eating anything; at least I try not to. In the United States there are notices in restaurants demonstrating the Heimlich manoeuvre and I recommend it.

Despite my pharyngeal pouch, I have been lucky and have enjoyed very good health, though I have had my fair share of accidents. For example, at the age of six I was sledging down a hill near our house headfirst when I misjudged something and ploughed straight into a fence at the foot of the hill. My nose was busted. My Uncle Jim, an ear, nose and throat doctor, mended it on our kitchen table.

On another occasion, I was down at some weekend conference when my appendix started to misbehave and I was whisked in an ambulance to Glasgow where it was quickly removed, fortunately without incident.

I've also nearly been swept away on the Tay, just gaining land by the skin of my teeth, and, once, driving home from Perth to Glasgow, a car swept from the other side of the road right into my car and I was left shell shocked. A police car swept onto the scene and I heard one of the police say, 'Call an ambulance.' This was the last thing I wanted to hear and I recovered sufficiently to protest. Eventually, a taxi was summoned to take me all the way to Glasgow. I had phoned Ursula and she arranged for Dr Carol Smith to be in attendance.

Fortunately, I was not in too bad a condition. I recovered all costs and damages from the unknown driver, who was charged, though I never learned the result. This has always struck me as odd. In Scotland, at least, the injured party is never told of the outcome of a criminal prosecution.

And I was hospitalised after falling at our friend Susan

Clements' holiday house in Western Australia in 2012. Lucky? I am certainly lucky, fortunate and happy to be alive. I still thank the many doctors and nurses who looked after me. Without them I would be a distant memory.

24

BRIDGE

Whilst bridge has been a passion of mine over many years, it was preceded by chess. But my chess career was strange. I played a little at school, but never enough to learn the moves and only vaguely knew the rules. When I was courting Ursula, I went over to Germany where her younger brother Hensel was staying with his parents. Our exchange of language was limited, but he produced a chessboard and I agreed to play him. He was many years younger than I was but beat me on three occasions. Needless to say I was mortified and humiliated and I vowed that that would not happen again.

What to do? Well, what does one do when ambition flares up and resolution sinks in? I purchased books, studied games and set out the chess problems in the evening paper on a board, or at least Ursula did that for me, so that when I came home from work the chess set was assembled with the instruction 'white to move and mate in three moves!' I found a local chess club and played there, losing, obviously, more often than winning, but gradually I got the hang of the game.

But I wanted more. I found out the name and address of one of the best chess players in England – Golombek – who was in the autumn of his life but still a great player. We were staying at that time in Gerrards Cross, about twenty minutes from London in the middle of Buckinghamshire, and cajoled the chess master (with a suitable fee of course) to come and teach us – Ursula and me – some of the rudiments of chess. He started by playing us a game simultaneously and, when he saw our standard, he clearly said to himself, 'There's work to be done here.' In any event, he persevered and I persevered and we became moderately good chess players – from the depths of nothing. Determination and hard work will usually pay off. And it did.

When the great Yugoslav Grand Master of Chess Gligorić, a world champion who won a chess Olympia Gold Medal in 1950, visited London, I was privileged to play him in a simultaneous chess tournament where he defeated us all, moving from table to table.

Ursula and I played for the club – although in my first game, which was supposed to last an evening, I was defeated by a young schoolboy after less than a dozen moves. But I have always been a trifle careless, if not reckless. Nevertheless, a salutary lesson.

But enough of chess. Contract bridge – a card game, originating from whist, is a magnificent game for the brain, which, while having an element of chance, allows the superior player to come out on top over time.

My learned father and my mother played bridge at home as a relaxation. I still remember as a youngster watching them play with Dr and Mrs Cranston for ten minutes or so each week. I watched, but did not follow the game. I just liked to study the expressions on their faces; the joy and the despair of the playing of the hand.

I had shown no interest whatsoever in the game, but could see that it fascinated others and that there was something one could learn from that fascination. But it was my brother Murray who introduced us to the game. We were on holiday with my brother and family and he had rented a house in Agay, a coastal resort on the Cote d'Azur. We needed something to do in the evening and I suggested we play whist, a game which I had tried occasionally and found remarkably easy to play – although not particularly well. Ursula entered into the spirit of this and the four of us would sit down and play Whist, then bridge. At home we invited one or two people who could play bridge and started to play with, and learn from, them. The fever caught hold of me and never departed.

My mother's new husband, James Clarkson, was a president of the Buchanan Bridge Club and it was arranged that they should give some lessons for beginners. Tom Glen was not a great bridge player, but a good instructor, and obviously read a book or two before each lesson. Also brought in was internationalist Bill Mitchell, an outstandingly good player. We both faithfully attended the lessons, learned a lot and became quite adept.

We duly applied for membership of the Buchanan Bridge Club, but in these days one had to have a test, which meant sitting with three committee members and playing two or three hands of bridge. I suspect the committee members were not really good bridge players and there was no trouble in gaining entry to the Buchanan Bridge Club. We donated a trophy, which we called the Mitchell Glen Trophy, for the most improved beginner and the classes continued. In view of the fact that we had donated the trophy, I decided it would be appropriate to win it, and luckily I did!

From then on there was no holding us back. I met and played with Jim O'Leary, an experienced player not really into bidding systems or conventions – a trait of most players of moderate ability who enjoy playing but do not want to put the work into refining and improving their game. O'Leary and I had agreed to play in the main Buchanan Championship, which extended over a whole year. I gave him the marked book and asked him to score out anything that he did not want to play, giving him his rightful place. He responded and marked the book (it must have been the first bridge book he had read in his life) and used his skills at dummy play and defence.

I was told by my sceptical stepfather that we had no chance and would be out after preliminary rounds. I was lucky in that, not only were we not out, but we were in the lead. When it came to the last day of the season, we had to win by a certain amount over the two favourites – John Cross, a lawyer, and Carol Dickel, the bridge correspondent of the *Herald* and an internationalist. We were narrowly pipped into second place but, nevertheless, for a beginner it was nothing short of a triumph, which, perhaps improperly, lives with me forever.

The Buchanan Bridge Club, although famous and perhaps the leading bridge club in its day, was extremely conservative. As I mentioned earlier, Jewish people were not allowed to join and I was suitably aghast. I was also told that I could not expect to play for the Buchanan first team until I had been a member for at least five if not ten years. This was not good news for an over-ambitious young man.

There were other bridge clubs and we eventually joined Benjamins, named after Albert Benjamin, an international bridge player of the highest standing. He had founded a bridge club for Jewish people, but Jews do not have the same dreadful habits of the other bridge clubs and they welcomed gentiles.

Ursula was immediately adopted by Albert Benjamin and was introduced to a number of others who were not only good bridge players but companionable. She still is very friendly with Barbara Kay who, with Joyce Benson, was a women's internationalist.

Our bridge progressed well and Ursula was selected to play for Scotland in the women's team. This was an international event where all the UK countries played against each other and, lo and behold, when Ursula was playing, they won a trophy. This was an extraordinary feat and one that will live with her forever – and deservedly so.

At Albert's Club, as it was known, I met with Willie Coyle, a bridge internationalist supreme. For some reason he adopted me and, although he could prove to be an exceptionally diffi-cult partner to play with – involving rudeness and, at times, humiliation – it was worth it because my bridge improved immensely.

When he played with me in serious events, we were once second in a national pairs and played several trials unsuc-cessfully for the Scottish team. When he played with other superior players I used to watch and learn; one is never too young nor too old to learn. The highest I managed to achieve in Scotland was to play twice for the West of Scotland. You can't win them all. Willie Coyle has left an indelible mark in my bridge life; but that was only the beginning.

When I became president of the International Bar Association in 1995 we moved to London and, when I could not play much bridge then, I was able afterwards to visit rubber bridge clubs. Rubber bridge is more a game of chance, with two pairs playing usually for money, as opposed to team bridge or duplicate bridge.

I met Martin Hoffman, an Auschwitz survivor, and we became good friends. He also adopted Ursula. But there was much more to London bridge than Hoffman. When we moved to London, Bernard Telcher and his wife Kitty adopted us as friends and introduced us to other players. One of the players Bernard introduced us to was Tony Priday, a most charming man married to the irrepressible Vivienne.

We were fortunate inasmuch as we were able to arrange bridge at the house. One of our guests on occasion was the great Boris Schapiro. He was involved in top flight international bridge with Terence Reese, one of our legendary and most notable bridge players and authors, and in one world championship they were accused of cheating by holding their cards in such a way that the number of fingers shown showed the number of hearts, which in bridge could be an exceptionally useful ploy in defence. There was a scandal when they were reported. The English team withdrew and there was a full board enquiry. Fortunately, both Reece and Schapiro, after investigation of all the hands involved, were found to be not guilty.

Schapiro was an extremely interesting man – a former Wimbledon tennis player, he came from Eastern Europe and was the owner of racehorses. He still played a lot of rubber bridge and occasional duplicate bridge. He played with Ursula, whom he called, 'the very best of the bimbos'. This accolade from such a great man still lives with her.

But my entry to the international scene came along with Paul Hackett, a serious international player who had twin sons – Jason and Justin – who played international bridge together. Hackett was a wily customer. A professional, his fees were not too bad and never increased over the years which we played – in bridge, the amateur pays the professional. Having said that, he was an incredibly mean, or perhaps thrifty, man.

He had managed to arrange a column for bridge in the *Sunday Express* and I agreed to act as his advisor/sub-editor.

The earlier articles were excruciatingly bad, to the point of being appalling, and I had to send him amendment after amendment to make the articles understandable, readable and, above all, grammatical. Eventually the pennies dropped and the articles became better, but I still scanned each and every draft most carefully for a period of possibly five years. Apart from public acknowledgement in his Christmas article, I received not even a cup of coffee for my efforts.

We played a standard American system which had been laid out for a fee by one of his sons, who was the theorist of the family. I still play the same system wherever I can. We had an interesting bridge career together and qualified to play in the seniors for England in a number of international events and, while I was always very much the junior partner, our scoring was reasonably good and sometimes very good.

Sometimes he was not available for senior international events because he might qualify for the main English team and I found myself with a variety of partners – including Victor Silverstone, Andrew Thompson and Peter Czerneski. Paradoxically enough, the more serious event brings out the best in me. Although I was by no means good, with the different partners we always acquitted ourselves reasonably.

Hackett always captained the team and one time he suddenly withdrew because he was called in to the Open Team. I found myself, as a relatively raw youngster, captaining the English team at some major European event. Fortunately, Tony Priday was in the team and did all the paperwork and leg work. Another member of the team was John Collins, now deceased, who was one of England's best ever players. He was playing with a friend and, after the first session, was so rude and forthright to his friend that the friend announced that he was going home the very next day. What was one to do? I decided to do nothing as the friend was not a great player.

But Tony Priday, with all his charm and influence, cast bread upon the troubled waters and the pair linked together again.

Playing with Silverstone, who was himself an excellent player, was my worst international experience. I blame myself because he wanted to change some of the system radically and I went along with his wishes. As a result, when I sat at the table I was more worried about forgetting the conventions which he had introduced than concentrating on the bridge. A lesson for us all. Be prepared.

With Hackett I played for the senior teams for England on about four occasions after qualification during lengthy trials. We always had a very good team and we won the trophy three years out of four. I comfort myself by saying that these guys are all professional and play bridge all their lives full time. Me, I am a friend, a bumbling but lucky amateur who fastens on to good partners and is always prepared to learn. I learned a lot from Hackett and will, despite his thriftiness, always be indebted to him. How he put up with me I still do not know. Perhaps it was the power of the chequebook!

When we moved to Perth, Australia, we continued our love of bridge, playing first of all at a local club in Dalkeith where Ursula and I acquitted ourselves quite reasonably, securing our names on the winner's noticeboard within three months of joining. And when we moved house to Peppermint Grove in 2012, we joined the Western Australian Bridge Club, which was much closer, larger and friendlier.

I linked up with an Australian, originally from Perth, who moved to London for many years and now lives in Sydney – Michael Courtney. He is a full-time professional and while most Australian professionals spend their time playing rubber, he is still good, albeit with a mind of his own, for conventions and additions (and subtractions) to the system.

I remember one time, at the beginning of our relationship,

we went to Darwin to a major Australian congress. Ursula was playing with Steven Burgess, another excellent player. There were three events altogether: Ursula won the first and I was second; we played in the teams together and we won and, in the third event, Michael and I managed to come first. Altogether a great week for the Harper family!

My bridge appetite was whetted once again. I played with Michael Courtney in a very good team in two trials – called play-offs in Australia. In the first we lost the final by one point. In the second, with a narrowly better team, we got knocked out in the quarter-finals. Courtney and I, the weakest pair by far (because I was the weakest and least experienced player), acquitted ourselves honourably. No blame could be attributed to us – certainly in the second trial.

My latest long-suffering partner is a delightful man called Jonathan Free. I play with him occasionally (not enough) locally and came close to qualifying in the Seniors trials 2015. If he can cobble together a good team, I plan to play in the next set of trials. Last chance saloon for the young Harper to play for Australia. Watch this space.

I have also recently started to play with a delightful man, Geoff Holman, who gives up his golf in inclement weather to pound the table with me. He has a delightful wife Fran and is coming for two days' fishing in Scotland. Geoff played for Wales and partnered Geoff Hurst and that great Welsh and Scottish internationalist Patrick Jourdain. It is a small world … especially in bridge.

To play in the World Championships in San Paolo, Brazil in 2009, one had to qualify in the top five of the European Championship. We were playing in the Seniors. Lo and behold, we were fifth equal and did not qualify because of a split tie. No San Paolo. No Brazil. And no World Championships. But Dame Fortune intervened and one of the European qualifiers dropped out and we were parachuted into the World Championships. And so, after the usual politicking, the team, composed of Hackett and myself, Gunnar Halberg and John Holland, David Price and Colin Simpson, won our way through the preliminary rounds. We found ourselves in the quarter-final and then the semi-final and, would you believe it, ended up in the final against Poland.

A World Championship silver medal was guaranteed but, of course, we were there to win a Gold Medal. A World Championship, even Seniors, is a dream for all bridge players. As usual, Hackett and I played for the first two stanzas, giving the next two to the experts. Our task was not to suffer too heavy a loss. Alas, in the first stanza we lost something like sixty imps, an almost overwhelming defeat. If we had lost another forty in the next stanza it looked like a long boat home.

But Dame Fortune smiled once more. Hackett and I reached slam in clubs. That is, we had to make twelve tricks out of thirteen, or at least I was the poor declarer and had to do so. The cause looked pretty hopeless. In the other room they made five clubs. If we had gone down in six clubs, we would have lost something like thirteen imps. If we made six clubs, we would have gained about the same. A swing therefore on one board of no less than twenty-six imps.

Well, Dame Fortune smiled on us yet again. The guy in front of me had pre-empted in diamonds and I placed all the other points with his partner.

Ever fearful, frightfully bold, I finessed having a singleton in one suit – a most unusual play. Lo and behold, it worked. I was missing four clubs, including the queen, and normally one would play to drop the queen. Again, I finessed. Dame Fortune continued to smile and I made twelve tricks. This was a time when the back was against the wall. A lessor mortal would have collapsed. Perhaps I should have. My skills cannot compare with the experts. The only thing I have in my favour is grim bravery, a relatively cool head and stout refusal to panic.

After that stanza we had reduced the deficit to thirty. Our teammates finished off the recovery. England, for the first time in the Seniors, had secured a gold medal!

A few weeks later I was in Partridges (a grocers' shop in London) and I picked off the stand a *Daily Telegraph*. As was my custom, I looked at the bridge article before deciding whether to buy the paper. The headline read 'England's Brilliance' and I did not think too much about it until I read my own name and saw my own six clubs reported by Tony Forrester, one of England's greatest players. Needless to say, I purchased several copies of the *Daily Telegraph* for the article. Along with a few other writings in various papers faithfully pasted by Ursula, it hangs in our bathroom to this day. And I still have a presentation in bronze by a chap called D'Orsi, which is, of course, in pride of place.

25

A Lifetime of Fishing

We started fishing as a family in the River Machrie in Arran where we went on holiday. I was six at the time and was the only member of the family who had caught nothing after a month, until the last day. Seventy odd years ago and I remember it as if it was yesterday. My mother helped me by throwing the worm into a pool and achieved a greater distance than I could manage. I took the rod. It was our last day. This was my last chance.

Suddenly the rod started to bend and a finnock (a young sea trout) took the worm. I squealed with delight, played it carefully, shouting at my brother who was netting it, and being upbraided by my mother for shouting. I landed the fish, which I eyed with pride all the way home in the steamer. The fish was hooked well, but not nearly as well as I was hooked.

My latest fish was when I had turned eighty. Ursula had gone to Africa with some girlfriends. I was free to fish and went to Exmouth, two hours away by plane from Perth. I hired a boat with the owner and an assistant and we trailed an array of flies, teasers streaming from six rods, three of which held hooks.

We started with a forty-pound swordfish then, lo and behold, a marlin. Excitedly played, excitedly landed, well photographed and returned alive to its natural habitat. From six to eighty – both in years and in weight, except the first six was in ounces and the next eighty in pounds.

My father was also hooked and linked up with other expert fishers, notably the owner of a bakery, Mr Lamond, who would go in to his bakery at four o'clock in the morning and leave three hours later to catch a train to the upper reaches of the Clyde. He used horse hair, which he plucked from passing horses, and a very small fly. When I was young I caught a fish on the dry fly and he said, 'When you catch a fish on the dry fly in the Clyde you have become an angler'.

Mr Lamond, as he was always called, even by my father, accompanied us on many fishing trips and, unhappily, drowned aged about ninety fishing in Loch Ness when his boat overturned in a gale. We fished in Loch Katrine and Loch Arklet and various other lochs, catching brown trout, usually about a half pound in weight, sometimes a little more, sometimes a little less.

But it was at Loch Lubnaig that I reached the zenith. We used to go out with three in the boat; my father fishing in the stern and my brother and I taking half an hour each in the bow, alternating between fishing and using the oars to keep the boat steady with the wind. It was my turn at the bow. I still remember the fly at the bob (that is the top of three flies) was a Soldier Palmer. After I cast in, the line disappeared down and down, the rod bent, the reel screamed. But my father, hard of hearing at the time, could not hear the reel and shouted at me to let the line out. We had all caught big fish before, but nothing like this monster.

My father soon realised that this was a mammoth fish and wisely took the rod. The fish jumped and my father shouted, 'It's a salmon!' Of course he was wrong. It was the size of a salmon, but was a brown trout. My brother took the oars and was instructed by my father to row up and down the loch to tire the monster out. Sage advice! I quivered in the bow. He concentrated on the fish and my brother watched. Perhaps it was at that time that I learned the art of delegation. The trout was slowly brought into the shore. I was despatched immediately to bring down a pair of scales and the fish weighed at over 6lbs. This was an extraordinary weight at that time. Our good friend Mr Lamond said he had never caught a brown trout of six pounds. And I was twelve!

We had an old box camera but no film. After all, there was a war on. When we arrived home I toured as many chemist shops as I could find but when I asked for film all I received were blank expressions. If we couldn't photograph the fish at least we could eat it. My grandmother came for tea. Now the fish was caught on a Sunday, the Sabbath for old grandmothers, and I was instructed to say that the fish had been caught on a Saturday. I'm not sure that she enjoyed eating a fish as old as that, but what could one do? Even ministers of the cloth can tell fibs in a good cause.

We had many adventures. We were invited up for a day's fishing at one of Lord Weir's family estates. Lord Weir owned an engineering factory and also had fishing rights on the River Ara near to which he had some sort of castle. I was young at the time, still in my early teens, and was given a promontory – three or four yards was sufficient to cover that narrow neck of the river. My father was taken up to the falls beat.

Within a few minutes, my shrill shouts were heard and the ghillie appeared as I was struggling with a salmon on a trout rod. Needless to say, it was an uneven contest. The salmon jumped a couple of times. I remembered to lower my rod and the salmon went this way and that way and eventually crossed the river and disdainfully let go of the hook.

Some ten minutes later I was into another salmon which went straight down to the bottom and became stuck. It must have wrapped the line round a stone, but determined efforts by the ghillie could do nothing and eventually the hook came away after a large boulder was thrown in. Such is life when fishing for salmon.

By about four o'clock in the afternoon the ghillie clearly wanted to go home. Again, I remember as if it was yesterday, he assembled a large rod, put on a large fly and went up to the top of the falls where he cast down. Within a minute, without warning, he had hooked a salmon which took him downstream and which he eventually landed. He repeated the process, but this time when it was landed I noticed that it was foul-hooked. My cries about that fell on deaf ears. The ghillie packed his rod up, put the salmon in the boot and said goodbye – probably receiving a good tip from my father.

The good tip I had was how to foul-hook salmon. That tip was not lost.

When I was a student, I found vacation employment in the River Borgie in the very north of Scotland. My father, not being so daft, made arrangements with the owner that he would drive me up and be given a couple of days' fishing. Well, we were to learn about Highland ways. We were told to report to the river without rods at a certain time but, lo and behold, other men appeared with large nets. They threw them into every pool in sight and cleaned out all the salmon.

This was not good news for the Harper family, who were to fish these arid and empty waters the next day – despite my father's shouted warning to me to let some of the salmon through the net!

But the young Harper, now an energetic student, was not to be foiled. We were living in a hut three or four miles up the river and a presence of someone living in the hut was usually enough to deter poachers, although we were supposed to walk the banks of the river for several miles each evening, which we rarely did.

However, back to Pater! He fished away in the falls pool, whereas I remembered the lessons from the River Ara and cast against the falls, allowing my line with probably a dozen flies all bunched up and lifting the line hopefully. A salmon and then another and then another and another.

My old man went home with a boot full of salmon and was very popular amongst his friends. Meanwhile, we had six weeks where, apart from digging peat, we read and read, sending away to Penguin for new books. We had to look after ourselves for food but, not surprisingly, all I bought at the local shop, some four miles away, riding in the pillion of the ghillie's motorcycle, were potatoes and mayonnaise. Why? Because every two or three days I would catch a salmon (the easy way) and we would gorge ourselves. I have not been able to look at salmon properly on the plate since that time.

I felt sorry for the poor fishers who had paid to fish after the pool had been netted, but a few weeks later the rain came and the salmon started to flow up the river again and I even caught one legitimately, which was of course taken by the ghillie for sale on behalf of the owner.

The apex of family fishing was on the River Ythen, for a good few years after the war. We stayed in Newburgh, some twelve miles north of Aberdeen and lived in a caravan with a tent beside it. The River Ythen was in the estuary which was salt water and tidal. One could only catch fish on the ebb tide, so we were able to spend time on the golf course. On the first one or two visits we noticed one man hook more than his share of fish and discovered that he had made his own minnows out of aluminium, which were lighter than other minnows made of lead and seemed to suit the tidal water.

My father, a great learner, learned from him how to make these minnows and, before we knew it, in the house we had set up various technical equipment to fashion minnows. The great advantage of which was that it had side hooks and sea trout normally attack minnow from the side as opposed to a salmon, which will come from behind. These were a great success, all the more so when we made them longer and put two side hooks on them, making them resemble sand eels, which the salmon loved.

The hotel – the Udny Arms – was too posh for the likes of us. The guests used to go out on boats with the ghillies at the oars, but we never saw them catch many fish and soon identified top taking spots from the bank. My brother and I shared a rod and we had many happy memories of fishing in the Ythen.

I stopped fishing during my courtship and for quite some years after marriage. When Robin was about six I was able to use him as an excuse to go fishing and, thus, we went together. I was lucky my brother had introduced me to the River Tay, which we could not afford as schoolboys. It was an expensive place to fish, but if one chose the dates and the locus carefully, one could get fish, especially in those days.

My first experience on the Tay was just after my brother had shown me how to fish the prawn and, indeed, how to dye the prawn. Of course I did it improperly as I put either too much salt in or too much water or too little dye and stank the house out boiling prawns. Eventually, I knew I had met my match and was able to purchase dyed prawns, and later shrimps, from George McInnes, of whom more later.

Armed with prawns, we went to Ballathie, in the middle reaches of the Tay, the finest part for fishing. We had one day with a group of Murray's friends. I remember I was down with an older man and we stood close to each other. He seemed to be catching salmon and I was not. I studied his methods, throwing the prawn very slightly upstream and then letting it trundle it down with a weight keeping it near the bottom. Eventually I got the hang of it and, in this one spot, I still remember it as if it were yesterday, we extracted more than a dozen salmon. In these days one kept all the salmon one caught. When we stopped for lunch, my brother and his friends on the other side of the river caught a few, but nothing like our bag. We were summarily ejected and told to fish elsewhere.

We found a spot further down and it was in that spot, after hooking and losing a few, that I caught my largest salmon – over thirty pounds! We finished the day with over fifty salmon. The ghillie could not believe it and neither could we. We've never had a day like it since, which is just as well.

But just as the salmon were hooked on the prawn, then so was I and I took Robin up to the stretch called the Benchil Beat where we had a great time. When I hooked a salmon I stayed out for a while until it was fairly tired then brought the rod in and handed it to Robin and he got his first taste of landing salmon. He must have been about eight at the time when he was fishing upstream from me. The ghillie was nearby and Robin hooked and landed his first salmon. I was overjoyed (and I suspect he was too).

My mentor in Tay fishing was the aforementioned George McInnes. He could catch fish where others would fear to tread. He had an incredible low gravity to cast away with water lapping round his waist – even in heavy currents. He was unflappable and the most brilliant fisher whom I have ever met. Naturally, I studied his techniques and copied them as far as I could. In these days my arrangement with McInnes, who was a policeman, was that I would pay for his fishing and he would give me two thirds of the salmon he caught. I am sure I was an outright winner.

We once obtained access to the Islamouth, the Rolls Royce of fishing, but fly only. On the first day, the ghillie was off so the old shrimp and prawn came out with great success, half of the catch being stowed in the boot, so when the ghillie returned he would not realise how many we had caught. Oddly enough, I was upstream as the 'lookout' and caught a fair number using the fly.

On the second day the ghillie, suspecting something was wrong, came early and caught one or two of us with shrimps on their hook. I quickly had managed to change over to a Devon, but all to no avail. The owner was phoned and we were told that we were ejected from the river and our salmon would be confiscated. Fortunately, Fred Berkley, who had arranged the trip, said that the cheque had not been cashed and he would stop it. This set them back and it was agreed that we would keep the fish, but we would stop fishing. I mentioned that I had not been fishing the shrimp and would therefore continue fishing.

I was allowed to for a while but then packed it in. The ghillie took out a notebook and officiously wrote our names in the book. He knew my name and he knew Fred's, but there was another chap who shall remain nameless who was unknown to him. When he was asked his name, he was about to give it, and I replied on his behalf, 'This is Mr Zavaroni.' The unnamed fisher caught on and was eternally grateful for his new name.

My former partner Lorne Crerar used to be my guest occasionally when fishing, as I was his. We once fished at Taymount at the end of a pool called Findford Head. My Devon (minnow) picked up a piece of line from the foot of the pool. It was lightly wrapped round my bait and I could feel a thump at the end. I knew that if I tightened up, the line would just come free. Lorne was fishing a short distance away and I signalled him up quietly. I raised the Devon with the line out of the water and we edged forward so that he could deftly wrap the line around the Devon in such a way that it would not come free. We had to do this very quietly and surreptitiously, otherwise the salmon would have moved away, never to be seen again.

When the line was secure, I lifted the rod to put pressure on the salmon which immediately bolted downstream through fast water and I had no choice but to run after it trying to make the bank safely as quickly as possible. Fortunately, there was a boat past the rapid water downstream, within which the ghillie could see my discomfort. He came to my aid and we played the fish from the boat for a long time – it was a big fish and I was put ashore.

But I could not reel in the line because of the obstruction of the Devon and some twenty or thirty yards of line after that. There was no alternative but for me to put the rod over my shoulder and walk back across a long stretch of sand and grass near the neighbouring woods and, from some thirty or forty yards away, I continued to play the salmon, eventually beaching it, where it was killed by others on the boat who had helped me. I suspect the fish was foul-hooked – judging from the way it played and the way it rushed downstream, but in these days a fish was a fish and the unwritten rule about returning a fish which was foul-hooked was conveniently ignored.

Another of my fishing guests was a world bridge champion, Geir Helgemo. I invited him, paid for his accommodation, got him a lift from the airport and gave him two or three days' excellent fishing, along with his then girlfriend. I even arranged for a salmon to be smoked and sent to Norway. And, of course, he did not have to discuss bridge during his fishing. Nobody knew anything about the game. To be selfish, I presumed that he would give me a game in some European championship. I have said hello to him since but am still waiting...

We still have a timeshare on the Tay for the first week in September. When I moved to Australia, the redoubtable Alastair Sheach took charge. An interesting chap and a great fisher, he owns a lawn mower business and I remember fishing with his father in the early days. He was an inveterate user of the Toby (a metallic heavy object) which he used to wing across the Tay, reaching distances to which no one else could aspire. We used to pack him off to the top of the beat so that we could be free for other gentlemanly pursuits. Before lunchtime Alastair had arrived at the bottom of the beat having covered the whole beat with his zooming Toby. Eventually, we had to split up the beat into two to make sure he kept in the top half of the beat for the morning or vice versa. Later, he took up other pursuits and became adept with the fly.

Now I had a fly rod for the Tay and, having cast all my early years with a trout rod, was able to get out a passable line – but not enough for the Tay. Accordingly, accompanied by Fred Berkeley (in his Rolls Royce) and John Mackay, we engaged a day's lesson with one of the world fly casting champions, Peter Anderson.

We went down to the Borders and he had a look at our fly-casting and decided that there was much to be done. He taught us how to overhead cast and spey cast. I was lucky inasmuch as, when casting a fly, I am ambidextrous, and enjoyed every minute of the lesson, resolving to get better and better. And this I did, even adding to the spey cast a double roll cast. I did not necessarily catch more fish with my expert casting – probably less – but I enjoyed it. The satisfaction of a beautiful cast cannot be beaten.

Fishing is not all about catching fish. It is the challenge, the company and, paradoxically, the solitude. My best memory to do with fishing is in Florida where, along with a friend, Jim Russell, we decided to go shark fishing. The first day, nothing, apart from a surfeit of sun and beer. The skipper did not like to be 'skunked', so we arranged a second day. Balloons on the surface. One popped and we arose expectantly. Unhappily the sun, not a fish, had done the damage but, near the end of the trip, a mammoth shark swallowed the bait. It was Jim's turn to play it, but I clearly remember being given a shot on the rod. It was massive and when it eventually tired, Jim gaffed it in. It was nearly the length of the boat. What now?

The boatman took out a rod like a thick walking stick and inserted a shot cartridge brought down suddenly on the head. Nothing happened. The same again – so I bravely put my head over the side, and then the shot fired and I was splattered. The shark was so big it could never have been brought aboard, so we made our way back with the carcass tied to the outside of the boat, and hung and weighed it with giant scales.

And what now? Eighty-one and still going strong. And I still own a timeshare. So here goes. Health permitting I go back to Taymount later this year. Shall not be wading up to my armpits in fast flowing water – I promise. My eldest son Robin is coming for the whole week. But he is getting on a bit as well! I suspect I may be nearing the end of my fishing days. But never say die. I might be able to return and return and return. You are only as old as you feel, and I am starting to get younger.

Give credit to the lure of the salmon.

26

ART FOR ART'S SAKE

My affection for art is, I suspect, historical. During the war, Kelvingrove Art Gallery deposited a number of paintings in private houses on the outskirts or beyond the city. We often visited the Kelvingrove Art Gallery when young. I remember the director, Dr Tom Honeyman – at one time a rector at Glasgow University when I was there – getting into serious trouble. Tom Honeyman had an unerring eye for great works of art and used most of the gallery's budget in one particular year in purchasing Salvador Dalí's *Christ of St John of the Cross*. It was a stunning picture and a number of us went to the gallery several times just to see and admire it. But needless to say, some critics fastened on to the price and complained. It is suffice to record that the sales of the postcards made from the picture's image more than paid for the painting itself. And I can only imagine what the painting might be worth today.

Tom Honeyman was a man ahead of his time. He introduced

my Uncle Jim, another doctor with a great art collection, to Leslie Hunter, another great Scottish artist, and my father owned two pictures by Hunter, which I eventually inherited. One was good, the other mediocre. Many years later I, somewhat stupidly and regretfully, sold them both.

My father had a large manse and, from the age of five, I looked at paintings – apart from the ones he owned. I do not recall them now, apart from one very large and somewhat gloomy painting by one of the Glasgow Boys – Robert Macaulay Stevenson. Many years later I purchased one of his paintings, which still hangs in our Perth house.

Just after I was married I wanted to buy a painting of my own and visited several galleries. What should I come across but a Hunter – a still life – for £120. I could not afford that at the time, but agreed with the owner that I could make monthly payments. To my shame, I did not keep up the payments in due and proper time and I still remember receiving a rather abrupt missive for my debt. Fortunately, I was able to discharge it.

No one else in the family particularly liked the painting, so eventually I sold it. When the family heard that I had sold it at Sotheby's Auction for £6,000, views changed radically. I attended the auction with my son Robin, probably aged about twelve at the time, and there came up for sale a William McTaggart. I bid for it, or at least Robin did on my behalf, and I bought it precisely for £6,000; so there was no profit or loss. I still have the McTaggart and it is absolutely splendid – a scenic of the west coast of Scotland.

I had previously started to build up a collection. My then partner Donald Dewar had inherited some fine paintings from his father (a doctor), and he was much more knowledgeable than me about Scottish art. We both attended Sotheby's sale at Glasgow Central Hotel and I decided to buy pictures for the office. With Donald Dewar's help, we bid for a number of paintings, all for different offices.

Having written a firm's cheque for the paintings, we were fortunate in some of our buys, but our auditors (Coopers & Lybrand as they then were) would not give tax relief for the paintings and advised that we would have to buy them individually. Being a decent sort of soul, I naturally sent circulars to all the other partners offering any partners paintings at cost. Fortunately, none responded.

Included in the Central Hotel sale was an alleged Landseer, a *Stag awaiting Removal, Partridge* by Thorburn, a head study by J.D. Fergusson (subsequently 'lent' to Donald Dewar) and *Fisherman* by Scott Naismith, still hanging in Perth. It was perhaps not surprising that none of the partners elected to buy. I paid a cheque to the firm and was left with a very interesting collection, some of which I still have.

I took counsel from Roger Billcliffe of the Fine Arts Society and Donald Dewar. I wanted to build up a Scottish collection and later, somewhat regretfully, sold a de Breanski. My art collection has been composed of both purchases and sales, each sale with regret.

I decided, after consultation, to focus on the Glasgow Boys and sought, but never managed, to secure a painting by each of them. At one time I had a Francis Cadell (one of the Scottish Colourists). In the middle of the painting was a black untidy scarf lying on a table. My eagle-eyed daughter Susan noticed this scarf, pointing out that it was the shape of a pelican's beak. After that, whenever I looked at the picture I could see nothing else but the scarf. I sold this picture and was surprised to see it some time later on the walls of Murray Johnstone, a large financial advisory house which was involved with us in the privatisation of Scottish Coal.

I used to attend auctions and, when it came to bidding for

the best pieces, I found that I was frequently outbid by the Fine Art Society, Billcliffe himself having an unerring eye, the auctions being frequently attended by his boss in London. Well, what to do? The answer was simple: rather than attend auctions (I could rarely spare the time and it was, in any event, a dangerous thing to do) I made an agreement with the Fine Art Society to bid for me on a commission basis – I think 10%. And this ploy worked. When they took a commission (and they could rarely refuse), I was spared the main opposition – and legally.

My greatest triumph came from the first auction at which they took a commission. The wording of the commission was that I would fix a maximum price and they would enter the auction and, if it went for lower than that, then all good and well.

In Glasgow I recall a McTaggart came up for sale; a great painting and I still remember the look of disgust when my man turned up, having purchased it for much less than my maximum price, and considerably less than the price he would have paid for it. This was a bit of luck; the picture was sold early in the auction when other professionals arrived late, having attended an earlier auction elsewhere on the same day. I bought this painting for about £5,000 and, many years later, could not resist an offer for it for some £90,000. The Art Society bought some other McTaggarts but would not sell them to me, even though I offered an immediate profit. I think they were vexed enough by me already – and understandably so!

I also turned to the Scottish Colourists: Hunter, Peploe, Fergusson and Cadell. I built a collection of them but, because of investments in Africa, reluctantly sold them. I do not have a Scottish Colourist left. Nevertheless, I made a goodly profit.

I had attended one auction myself with Donald Dewar for

the sale of an impressive number of paintings from the estate of industrialist Robert Wemyss Honeyman. Pieces were, on the whole, extremely good and the bidding was intense; well above my range. I remember nearly falling asleep during the auction, having absented myself from the bidding at a very early stage. Then suddenly, lo and behold, one of the last items was a Peploe. The bidding seemed to die very early on. Prompted by Donald Dewar, I stuck up my hand at £6,000, confident that I would be outbid and I could drop back to my reverie. Suddenly, I found myself the owner of this painting and poorer by £6,000.

I was extremely nervous and took the painting back to the office. I loved it but Ursula was not quite so enthusiastic. Nevertheless, we hung it and it gave me considerable joy for quite some years, that is until sometime later an art dealer offered me some £90,000 for it. How could I refuse?!

Some time later, I was visiting the Belgravia home of Irvine Laidlaw, later to become Lord Laidlaw. When I was sitting in his lounge discussing some business or other I looked up, gasped, pointed to the picture and said, 'Hey, that's my painting!' Needless to say, he was surprised and I told him the background – but not how much I had paid for it! That might have spoilt his day.

I once attended an exhibition by Roger Billcliffe of a significant artist (now deceased), Sir Robin Philipson. He was there himself. Philipson every year produced one or two paintings of poppies and I thought that they were very rich and extremely viewable. I accosted him, in a friendly manner, and asked if he would take a commission for a painting of poppies with a legal theme. At first he demurred, but when I offered to buy one of the paintings on the wall, he weakened and agreed to take the commission.

He only painted the poppies at a certain time of the year

(understandably) and I left the choice of legal theme entirely up to him; one does not interfere with great artists. After he painted it, it was hung in an exhibition in Bristol before I received it. At the top of the painting are two small reproductions of French lawyers by Daumier and, at the foot of the right-hand side, a sketch of Don Quixote on his horse, Rocinante. I just wonder if that contained a hidden message about me?

Although I sold my Colourists, I still have in my room three Hornells, a Philipson and a McTaggart. It must be one of the most splendid rooms in Perth. Ursula's room has a couple of Peter Howsons and a painting I bought for her, even though I said that I'd hung up my wallet.

She had gone with a friend, Susan Clements, to Melbourne to an art show – a dangerous venture – and came back raving about a painting titled *It Happened After the Rain*. This showed two girls looking in a puddle, seeing their reflection, with real photography of motor cars in the background – a photo print, acrylic and water-based paint on canvas.

I was told by Ursula the price was about $10,000. Since we had no Australian art in the house, and Ursula was so fond of the painting, I agreed hastily to purchase it. Well, it was already purchased – by Ursula! But more was to come; the actual price was over $18,000 with transport of another $2,000 or more.

Yet worse was to come; the artist was not Australian. The painting is by a Japanese lady called Rei Sato. Not to worry, the painting is beautiful and gives Ursula much pleasure. It goes well with a couple of small Howsons and a Mary Armour. The Mary Armour is a gorgeous still life I bought when the artist was still alive. A van full of Mary Armours was touring a number of offices and I was captivated by it, but not as much as Ursula; she adores it and keeps it in her room, along with

The Road Man by Gemmell Hutchison, depicting a weary man walking along the road. She says it reminds her of herself!

We each have in our rooms a statue by Benno Schotz, one of the Queen's sculptors. I met him by chance in the 1960s and purchased two sculptures, both of which, in my untutored view, are outstanding.

But who is the daddy of them all? Undoubtedly Peter Howson. He was one of the new Glasgow Boys and prolific in his output, starting off mostly with large domineering Glasgow figures. I met him at one of his exhibitions in the 1970s and persuaded him to do a large painting with a legal theme so that it could it hang in our then new offices at the Ca' d'Oro in Glasgow. Some years later it was finally produced, *The Kangaroo Court*, a beautiful, but menacing, painting. It still hangs in the Ca' d'Oro. I sold it to the office at cost price of about £7,000, but it is now worth more than twenty times that amount.

I got to know Peter Howson very well and helped him in some of his troubles (he has always had an uneasy relationship with agents). I managed to obtain some smaller paintings, including the original painting for a 'stamp' which he used, although, if I recollect correctly, it was somewhat criticised as the Queen's head was in smoke!

In my hall I am met by three stunning Howsons. The first is of Jacob fighting with the Angel, the second is of a fight in the Cuillins and the third is the Age of Solitude. They still give me immense pleasure and, in the hall itself, Ursula has framed a number of Christmas cards which Howson drew individually for the lucky recipients. In my room I have a very early Howson of a boy crouched against a Glasgow wall. I have a number of his other paintings, too numerous to mention, all of which give me delight when I pass them.

But if Howson was the daddy of them all, the mummy

of them all is my niece Alison; a lovely girl, married to a Kenyan with a grown-up young son. She is the only artist in the family. Where she acquired her skills I have no idea but I do recall her graduation exhibition at the Glasgow School of Art, where some of her paintings were hung. She was going to be a struggling artist and my eyes went quite moist when I saw her work. I seem to remember making her eyes a trifle moist by producing a pocketful of cash, or it might have been a cheque. Since then we have been given, and occasionally purchased, a number of Alison's paintings, which hang throughout the house.

A good painting so lifts the spirits – even one which I somewhat unwittingly paid a record price for: a Pirie (one of the Glasgow Boys) which hangs in my room and features nothing other than a strutting cockerel with no background, but art for art's sake.

I have now given some of the pictures to the children. Are they good? Well, they must be. Otherwise I wouldn't have bought them!

27

VICES

My recent medical, or rather dental, ban on smoking coincided with a mammoth Australian government campaign. Indeed, my local paper ran a story recently headlined 'Cigarettes running out of puff', reporting that nearly two fifths of Western Australians support a total smoking ban and more than half want taxes on tobacco increased. This is after the world's toughest tobacco packaging laws were upheld in a court recently. Advertising on the harmful effects of smoking seems undoubtedly to be having an effect but, oddly enough, as a smoker, I am in favour of the campaigns.

I have admitted I am a smoker. Ursula is too. My parents smoked and so did her father. Fortunately, our children do not want to smoke and, to our knowledge, their children have not dabbled. Quite right. How did our cravings start?

I was raised in a smoking house. Indeed, when we went on caravan holidays and all slept under the one roof, my parents smoked – albeit keeping the windows open. In the car they would smoke too – I still remember my mother in the passenger's seat every so often lighting up a cigarette for my father, who was driving. This must have been in the days before they had cigarette lighters.

When I was about seven some of our friends came round to our loft above the garage in the old manse. A woodbine and a match could be purchased for a ha'penny. I never took more than one puff, understandably. My brother started smoking in his teens, but I was above that. I still remember his face when he crouched over the fireplace with a fag in his mouth when my parents returned unexpectedly. He avoided being caught – but just.

But why did I start? Fortunately, I have never smoked cigarettes. I knew about the dangers of the damage caused to the lungs. My father's and mother's coughing was not pleasant, although my mother lived well into her eighties. As did her mother, and she smoked too.

One of my vacation jobs when I was at university was near Grantown-on-Spey. We worked at Revak Lodge as students and would stay in the stables and beat for grouse for the wealthy. Depending on the quantity of grouse, we would work for three or four days a week and, armed with a flag, would be sent out into a large semi-circle. We then sat down on the heather till the guns took their leisurely place behind the butts a mile away. Waiting, sprawled on heather on a rain-free day, and being paid for it, sounds quite like paradise; but every paradise has its problems, and ours was the Scottish midge, which paid no respect to hardworking students and invaded like stormtroopers!

Yet one of my fellow students remained impervious and untouched. Why? Smoke from his pipe drove the devils away! I decided there and then that it was a pipe for me. Well, I went to Grantown, some twenty minutes' walk, and purchased my first pipe and a tin of Dobie's No. 7 tobacco. I enjoyed it and the midgies hated it. I was duly comforted.

When I became just a little wealthier, I adopted different types of pipe and different tobacco. I had tried a black thick shug, but it was far too strong for me. Eventually I was able to move to Sobranie, the Rolls Royce of pipe tobaccos. In these days we could smoke anywhere. I remember once smoking in the corridors of a court, waiting for the case to be called. Suddenly it was called and I put my pipe in my pocket, having tamped it gently with some instrument. When I was in the middle of cross examination I felt my whole jacket become exceptionally hot and realised the pipe in my pocket still had some burning ash and I was nearly aflame. I felt like shouting 'fire, fire!' and causing an evacuation of the courtroom, but I was able to avert potential catastrophe by banging the pocket and extinguishing the fire.

I had several pipes, some of them pretty expensive. The reason I had so many pipes was that I hated cleaning. I bought special cleaners and sometimes I took a number of pipes into tobacconists for a professional cleaning. The whole job of cleaning a pipe with a scraper was both dirty and distasteful.

I was by then smoking a lot and this was taking its toll on my mouth and throat. Nothing serious, but when I woke up in the morning my whole mouth sometimes seemed furry. This persisted and one morning I woke up with a typical furry mouth and picked up the pipe from my side table (I had been smoking in bed the night before) and purposefully broke the pipe in two. I have not smoked a pipe since. Horrible dirty things, as Kipling once remarked.

When I was in my forties I stopped smoking for around ten years and, with the persistence and advocacy of a non-smoker, tried to persuade Ursula to stop. She smoked cigarettes during the day and even at the bridge table when, thinking of a bid she should make, she would light up a fag. However, the mind was willing but the body was not and frequent promises have thus far come to nought.

Bribery was worth a thought. So I bribed Ursula with a full-length black mink coat no less. This was gratefully and immediately accepted and she duly gave up – for three full days. Eventually, in one of her conservation moods, she gave this horrifically expensive garment to her close friend Steff.

Other bribes were also in vain. Finally, she wanted a car. 'Would you give up smoking?' I asked.

'Gladly,' she replied. I bought the car, a lovely Daf, and her smoking stopped … for a full two weeks.

When I gave up pipe and cigar smoking, one of the benefits was the absence of the reek, although alcohol can be just as bad. I remember the story of Lionel Daiches, a very successful and talented advocate specialising in criminal law on minimum preparation. His talent shone through. He enjoyed a drink and, one day we had a consultation in Barlinnie Prison after lunch. He undoubtedly had a regal lunch and I drove him to the prison, a mile or two outside Glasgow. He conducted a consultation with one of my clients prior to a High Court criminal trial. As usual, he had not particularly studied the papers but his elegance, poise and knowledge impressed the client. Or seemed to. As he said, cutting the consultation short as he always did, 'Any questions, my good man?'

'I have no questions Mr Daiches,' replied my client, 'but just breathe on me once more.'

After years of refusing cigars at dinner functions (and they were free), I surrendered and started the occasional cigar, then the not-so-occasional cigar and then, of course, the regular cigar. But the price of good cigars in Australia is shocking. Even worse than the UK, and that's saying something.

I have smoked for the greater part of my life, as has Ursula and her parents. Do I advocate smoking therefore? No. A resounding, positive, definite NO! I comfort myself that, as a cigar smoker, I do not inhale smoke, which is apparently bad for the teeth and plays riot with the gums and will invade the lungs. My dentist would like me to stop and, of course, he is right. But I am enormously lucky as I am in my eighties and, like Johnnie Walker's whisky, am 'Still going strong.' But not all of us are lucky and, frankly, I do not deserve to be. Whenever I meet a reformed smoker I mentally doff my cap in sheer admiration.

In my opinion, countries are absolutely right to try to limit smoking as much as possible through increased taxes and smoke-free restrictions. All to the good, though I am not sure whether the anonymous packaging is a success or not; those who smoke will smoke regardless of the packaging.

As for a total prohibition? No, definitely never. It would be like alcohol prohibition in the States: impossible and impractical to enforce. But smoking is decreasing in popularity so something is working. And that, says an inveterate cigar smoker, and a former pipe smoker, is all to the good.

And as for that other great vice, gambling, I used to say that I might gamble on horses if I ever saw poor bookmakers. No troubles there; no gambling! But, of course, lawyers gamble all the time; they gamble that the fee may eventually be paid.

Has anyone not gambled in their past? I certainly have. At our tennis club we used to play pontoon (black jack) with matchsticks, with some of the older boys playing poker for real money. I watched a game one day and one boy was clearly very experienced. I watched as another became poorer and poorer, losing a series of games, going paler and more and more humiliated. I did not know much about poker, but I could see that it was not just a game of chance, but a real skill. Not for me.

And I remember when backgammon swept the country and was played in the bridge club in Glasgow for money. Some of the members were not working and not only played backgammon continuously, but studied the game. The rest of us might dabble, but I quickly realised that it was a game of skill and appreciated that the occasional player would have no chance against the semi-professional. Not for me – thank you very much.

Not long after marrying, when I lived briefly in Buckinghamshire, I met a mathematician who told me about the odds in roulette. He said that he had calculated the odds of twelve blacks or twelve reds in a row. While each throw has a 50% chance individually, when the odds were calculated in a number in a row, they were changed significantly. A system was to visit the roulette table and wait for a run of red or blacks – say four – he would then place a bet on the colour which had not come up four times in a row and, if it came up five times, he would double the bet so that he was betting against it six times in a row and keep on doubling. He argued that he was bound to win – there was no limit on the stakes. He warned that it also required patience to wait for a suitable run to come up, which would not be frequent. What sounds too good to be true usually is.

With my brother Murray and family, we had rented a house in Agay in the South of France and one day we trooped into the casino at Nice. I had a fair bit of cash and I had a system. For a while my pickings were small. Perhaps I became a little bit impatient. In any event, I started my doubling, doubling and doubling and numerous reds or blacks came up in a row. I don't know whether the table was rigged or I was spotted or whether I was just unlucky. Lucky or not, I was broke and, indeed, I think I had spent the return taxi fare.

I had one token left. It was a bit of a waste of space in the pocket. However, with a look of despair, I put it on a single number. Would you believe it? Dame Fortune now smiled and let my single number come up – a thirty-even to one shot! And enough to get home. I had, however, been sufficiently alarmed and now rarely venture a penny in a casino. In fact, I have rarely ventured into a casino; although I did enjoy watching high stakes being played by high rollers.

I have known a number of good solid citizens being driven to despair because they thought they could forecast tips from stable boys, trainers or newspapers. When I was a legal apprentice, my former boss, Jimmy Martin, was a rough diamond, but extremely pleasant. He once regaled us with a story of how he was a youthful car attendant at a racecourse. When people parked their cars, he would give them a tip. He would pick out a race in which there were six or more horses running and when someone parked he would sidle up to them and whisper the name of a horse and say, 'Back it. It's going to win.' And so on. He gave the next car owner another horse and, indeed, tipped them all to win, making sure he remembered which car he had tipped so he could identify the winner when he came to his car. I don't know whether he made very much from returned tips, but I found the story and the technique interesting and it has stuck with me for fifty-five years.

I claimed that I did not gamble on the horses and this is true, but a concatenation of events broke the rule with not, I am afraid, a happy ending. It all started with the fishing; two Englishmen had rented a week in one of the best beats in the middle part of the Tay, where I loved to fish. Thanks to my policeman friend, George McInnes, I was given a day where there was a rod spare. The two Englishmen were 'slagheap millionaires' and one of them said that the next day he was going to the racecourse in Ayr to watch his horse run.

Being a polite sort of chap, who was there as a guest, I expressed interest, thinking it might just be an old nag and that this was a hobby entered lightly. He did, however, say the rider was Lester Piggott and that immediately got my attention. I know nothing about racing but had, as everyone had, heard of Lester Piggott. I was mightily impressed. He told me that the name of his horse was Regal Tack. I then wondered whether I should put some money on the horse in an each way bet. If the horse won, I would gain money. If it lost, he might feel that he owed me a favour and would invite me fishing again! This was evidence of my odd sort of thinking which has sometimes served me well in the past.

Well the next day I was up bright and early and was attending Kilmarnock Sheriff Court for a trial. My trial disappeared when a plea of guilty was negotiated and I took the car home to have lunch with Ursula, after which, before beating it back to the office, I picked up a *Glasgow Herald* and looked at the racing information. Sure enough, I saw at the racecourse Lester Piggott riding Regal Tack, owned by our slagheap millionaire friend.

What to do? I had never been in a bookmakers in my life, although I used to act for plenty of unlicensed bookmakers in the days before gambling became legal. In fact Jimmy Martin, my rough diamond boss as an apprentice, used to go out for lunch with the illegal bookmaker every so often and represented bookmakers who were arrested.

In these days the bookmaker would bail out the clients from police custody and they would never appear for any trial, the bail was forfeited and everybody was happy. When Martin, nicknamed 'Slash Martin', returned from these lunches, he would be clutching a large cigar and had clearly had a modicum of whisky. He used to prowl up and down the office smoking his cigars and wondering aloud, 'That was a great lunch – I wonder how the poor live?'

In any event, I decided to phone my bridge club, which is situated exactly above a bookmakers near the Sheriff Court, and spoke to Martin Jacobs, the manager, who, like most of the bridge club players, bet regularly himself. I explained that I had met the owner of a horse and that I would like to place some money on it. Would he do the needful? 'No problem at all,' he said. 'How much?'

Well, I had no idea, but I did want either to win a lot or go fishing the next year so I quickly said £100. In these days that was a fair bit of money and I could hear his intake of breath.

I then went back to the office, thought no more about it, and ploughed through the usual mountain of work. The race had been at 3pm and I had heard nothing from Martin Jacobs. I suspected bad news. I could not contain my impatience, however, and phoned him at 5.30pm to get a raspberry over the phone. The horse had not won.

What made matters worse was that Martin Jacobs had been so impressed that I had made such a bet, that he thought the information must be sound, that he himself put £50 on the ill-fated nag. No wonder he blew a raspberry over the phone!

I presented this story to the owner the following year, but there was no apology. Instead, he merely alleged the horse had been pulled. What is the motto of all this? Never bet. It's a mug's game. There are enough mugs in the world without adding to their number.

28

CHILDREN & GRANDCHILDREN

We moved to London in 1964, staying in a rented flat in Malvern Court, South Kensington. Ursula became pregnant and we were both over the moon.

Unhappily she started bleeding and I whisked her to a doctor a few floors below. No problem, he claimed. I shall scrape it all out. Ugh. Double ugh. But I had a brother, a doctor and professor. A phone call to him, and one from him, brought a specialist to the door. And after rest everything became fine again and Robin – would you Adam and Eve it? – was eventually happily and healthily born.

We eventually moved to Repton (Gerrards Cross) when he was an inquisitive toddler. We later moved to Glasgow so that I could resume the practice of law and that is where Robin grew up. He went to Sunday school under our tutelage, but that did not last too long. Robin had his own ideas about God and the after-life. At that time, we were staying in a small villa in Largie Road in Newlands.

But where religion was a 'no', fishing was a positive 'yes'. Robin used to come with me at the age of five or six when I took up fishing again and happily paraded around the banks of the Tay wearing red wellingtons and a waterproof jacket. He was entranced and eventually I let him play salmon, which I hooked, making sure that I stood out in the river until the salmon was truly tired and then handed the rod to Robin. Soon he took up fishing himself and, unhappily, I was half a mile down the river when he hooked and landed his first salmon. Fortunately, the ghillie was present.

I have not such good memories about the first salmon which he hooked on the fly. We were fishing in Stobhall and he caught a fish in one of my favourite spots – the Cubby Hole. Unfortunately, the salmon were round a promontory and I waded out to my waist, having taken the rod and engineered the salmon round, brought it in and handed the rod back to Robin on the bank. Most unfortunately, this single event will live with me for the rest of life. The salmon, when it was near the bank, jumped. I went to ensure that Robin dipped the rod, but my hand caught it and pulled it up and the salmon said 'thank you very much', landed with a splash and broke the line. Robin did not seem to be as frustrated as I was.

I remember once fishing the fly down to a taking spot at Taymount and, as my fly came round at the precise spot, I saw a salmon come to the surface and waited in expectation. Long could I wait because Robin, behind me, had let out his shrimp right down to where my fly was and hooked the salmon. Naturally, I pretended to be pleased. We landed it, but I still scratch my head at this young poacher. I don't think he has fished since the one time he went out from Sydney in a boat, but he was a dedicated, resourceful and successful angler, mixing exceptionally well with other guests.

He was good at school. There was one pupil there who

we called Conkie, who was even better, but this did Robin no harm to have stiff competition, otherwise things would become too easy. At school he was very interested in computers and wanted me to buy one. I had a better idea: I went into a computer shop and discovered that one could make a computer (or what passed these days for a computer). Once a week we went into the shop to buy different parts and Robin's handiwork would be approved or corrected. Eventually, after much labouring, he made his computer – although I'm not sure what it could do.

In any event, Robin passed his exams well and wanted to go to university. He decided that he liked science best of all and wanted to become a scientist. In no way would he become a lawyer. I had a brainwave. I invited him to visit my brother, who ran a medical research centre and who introduced us to some scientists.

My brother disclosed that the scientists all held first-class honours degrees from excellent universities, sometimes Oxford or Cambridge. When I asked what they were paid, he admitted they were paid a third of his salary: there was no money for scientists in the medical profession. A change to a computer science degree it had to be – and then I had another brainwave (I have lots of them and most of them are rubbish, but this one turned out to be a winner).

Strathclyde University – where I held a part-time post – had agreed to take in Robin on a science degree at the age of sixteen. I found out that in the science degree you are required to do two arts subjects and discovered that law subjects qualified. Accordingly, I persuaded Robin for his two non-science subjects to do law and spoke to my friend, Campbell Burns, who was then head of the Law School. The Law School obviously rather liked this possible influx of science undergraduates.

And lo and behold, Robin excelled at the two legal subjects, becoming top of the class. More importantly, he began to develop a liking for the law, which he had always eschewed (because of me I suspect). After that, getting through the regulations was downhill. I persuaded Campbell Burns to alter the rules so that a science graduate could enter the Law Faculty and – this was most important at the time – that if they get a first-class honours degree in science with two legal subjects, they could graduate in two years instead of the compulsory three years.

I still remember anxiously waiting on Robin's university results. A secretary gave me heart failure once by saying that Robin had phoned and she had thought the message was that he had failed. I was not good in court that afternoon, but then Robin came into the office proudly announcing that he had achieved a first-class honours degree. Marvellous news. I suspect he took his brains from his grandfather.

Robin sailed through his degree and obtained an apprenticeship in London. There was no question of me recommending him to join my law firm; that would have been a fate worse than death for him and he readily understood and concurred. He moved down to London and completed a successful apprenticeship, during six months of which he was seconded to Australia. And that was the beginning of the end. He fell in love with Australia. After his apprenticeship, he took a job with another major firm in Hong Kong, where we visited him, and then it was on to Australia.

When he was in Australia in 1995 we received an alarming phone call that he was seriously ill with a possibly life-threatening fever and had been lying in his bed unattended. He was eventually saved and he gives credit for this to his future wife, Kate, a hard-working and protective Sydney solicitor. He soon resumed employment with Mallesons, a major legal firm in Sydney and elsewhere.

Later, Robin announced that he was going with a pal to a finance company. I had a little input to this inasmuch as I introduced them to Deutsche Bank. In any event, they set up some sort of advisory financial business and seemed to make tons of money. Fortunately Robin moved on, retiring early. A wise move as his former partners did not fare well, with one of them ending up in jail.

Fortunately, Robin had some of the old man's tenacity and did not give up entirely on life and its challenges. Although he dedicated more time to war games and running three delightful children to school and the like while his wife worked as a lawyer, he decided to do a PhD on computer theory and in this he was successful (as my father was). He has enrolled for another PhD, although I have taken it upon myself to suggest that he shouldn't really do two PhDs and could he not change that to a different degree? He has now found some advisory work. Whether well paid or not, I don't know. And still studying for the second PhD – PhD squared!

Susan is the second child. We were living in Gerrards Cross when she was born – August 1966 – and her birth was without too much difficulty and she had the usual childhood (if there such a thing).

Unfortunately, when we returned to Glasgow, aided and abetted by her mother, she fell in love with horses; or rather ponies. I remember taking her to a riding school and sitting rather uncomfortably on a horse myself while little Susan trotted beside me on a small pony. She was given lessons and shown how to jump.

There was no holding back Susan, which was no great help to my bank account because, as she became more adept, the ponies became more expensive and the competition more intense. Eventually, I am happy to say, from jumping horses she went into show ponies and we used to travel around the country. The kitchen was soon full of rosettes of all colours and Susan progressed with more expensive ponies. She won the Scottish Championship; for which I take a little credit. Ursula looked after her and the ponies but, at one qualifying event, for some reason Ursula couldn't manage and I took Susan up north, where she won and that sealed her Scottish Championship – probably forgotten by all but me.

I didn't go to every show, but still remember that on one occasion at Falkirk a large, well-known guy had parked his Rolls Royce next to our horse box and kept the engine running, thus making it difficult for the ponies to get out. I approached him by rapping on his window: he was a big fellow and clearly annoyed that I should touch his Rolls Royce. He moved to get out of the car, towering above poor little me. What was I to do? This was a battle which I could not win, yet I had to stand up for the rights of our ponies. Fortunately, Falkirk is adjacent to Polmont, which has a youth prison. Before I knew it, we were surrounded by half a dozen 'young stewards' who recognised me and saw that I might need some help. They circled round the man and, when learning of the problem, 'persuaded' him to move his Rolls, so that I was saved by former clients and Susan could get her horses out of the box. One up for Father!

I was somewhat gobsmacked when I learned much later that Susan, after I left for the office when she was dressed for school, was not always at school but often away to the stables with the ever-present caring mother while school got a miss. We sent Susan to a very posh school, Park School, and I used to drive her there in the mornings, pointing out, to her chagrin or boredom, the beautiful leaves on the trees as they changed each month. When we moved to Pollokshields, we decided it would be more sensible that she went to neighbouring Craigholme School, and this she did for a while. She then found that some of her friends at a farm in Newton Mearns went to Eastwood, which was a free school, and wanted to go there. Although ever careful of the wallet, I counselled against it but agreed. In the event, Susan lasted in that school for about two weeks, where the language and the smoking was just too much for her tender lungs or ears. What to do? Rather shamefacedly, I phoned Craigholme School and they said that they would welcome her back and, indeed, had expected her to return.

I had bought a house some distance outside London for the kids in 1989 in a location chosen by Robin – Leytonstone. The house was sufficient, I thought, for students. Susan stayed with Michael and Robin there for some time, but soon became restless. She landed a job in London with the law firm Clifford Chance. I had also bought a one-bedroom flat in London, at Cromwell Court in Chelsea in the early 1980s, which I didn't view before buying it, but had despatched Gordon Banks, the accountant, to do the needful. This flat was rented out, but when a tenancy came to an end, Susan, as only Susan could, grabbed the opportunity with both hands and insisted that she stay there. What could a poor father do?

The rest is benign history: at Clifford Chance she met David. She lived with him briefly in Cromwell Court – changed days since when I was a boy – and, later, had the marriage of the century at Stirling Castle in 1996. Where else could one find for a marriage to one's favourite daughter?

And I have to say it was a great success. Douglas Alexander, my schoolboy friend, was invited to come out to Stirling and conduct the wedding. He even dressed up in a kilt. We had Highland shows in the grounds, where some extras from *Braveheart* showed off their skills. We have one superb wedding photograph with Michael Forsyth, Secretary of

State for Scotland, Elizabeth Smith (John Smith's widow) and Donald Dewar, my former partner and Shadow Secretary of State for Scotland.

Eventually, Susan and David left Clifford Chance and moved to the Cayman Islands in 1997, securing employment in a major law firm before David, as many lawyers now seem to do, decided to retire early and move out to his hometown of Perth in 2010. Susan wouldn't go without her mother. Her mother wouldn't go without her husband and so here I am in Perth. The good news is that we are next door to Susan, David and the children.

When we decided to adopt an African child, we went out to a home near Glasgow in 1971 and took out a two-year-old, very quiet, subdued lad on a drive. We did this over several weeks before finally applying and receiving adoption, having been inspected severely by an adoption agency. When he was young, Michael seemingly had a talent for driving everyone off their rocker. I think he nearly drove the primary school teacher mad, and I'm sure she almost had a nervous breakdown. But good sense will prevail and eventually things settled down (or at least we heard less about his daily progress through the patience of his teachers).

We decided, after taking much advice, that the best thing for Michael would be to send him to boarding school and this, I think, was successful. The boy came good and, after settling down at Bedales school, he obtained entry to London University where he graduated with a law degree.

Michael obtained an apprenticeship with a major firm. All he had to do was pass some preliminary exams, which should have been a doddle compared to university (in fact Susan and Robin had taken them while still working). But, for reasons still not entirely understood to this day, Michael managed to spend a great deal more time on the sports fields rather than on syllabus study, necessitating a change in career path. From rugby union to soccer back to rugby union (and league) to American football (and back to rugby again), the family has always supported his enthusiasm for sports. I personally think he just had such an aversion to the law that he didn't bother his rugby boots. And perhaps he was right: after a spell working London and Edinburgh he decided to move to Sydney, Australia in 2000.

Michael never really took to fishing. I recall one time when he was young taking him out on a loch to show him how to fly fish for trout. I still remember to my delight, he was lifting his cast out of the water ready to make the next one when a trout had risen to the fly and the strike, although not intended, was perfect. The trout was landed, Father was happy and took the trout home in the car to be savoured. Unhappily, however, the car was stolen after I got home and the trout disappeared. The car was returned, I am told, by a young thief who discovered that it belonged to the criminal lawyer, Ross Harper! But no fish.

Michael came up occasionally to the Tay, but didn't take to it. I do recall, however, once when I was showing him how to cast a minnow in a pool in Benchil. He cast the minnow out and it went upstream and I shouted to him that this was wrong. What happens if the minnow goes upstream? It sinks and is stuck in a stone and perhaps lost forever. In any event, the minnow did stop and I started to shout at Michael. Suddenly, the stone on which I thought he was stuck started to move and, before you knew it, a salmon was dancing at the end of the line! Michael played it well and pulled it in. One for the pot. But did that glue Michael on to fishing? Certainly not. I doubt whether he has bothered with a rod in his hands since. But his father was pleased.

Michael is currently in a good job and recently enjoyed a six-month sabbatical. He has met a delightful girl called Helen, who is a lawyer. She has taken time off to be with Michael and they toured America. This, for the anxious parents, is nothing but good news and I do hope that we welcome the lovely Helen into the family. And who knows, Michael may become a father and we may have more than seven grandchildren.

Our seven grandchildren (so far!) are: Susan and David's children Nisha, Ross, Natasha and Marcus; and Robin and Kate's kids, Imogen, Harriet and Hamish.

Born in London in 2003, Nisha spent her first seven years living there. She loves and excels in maths, evidenced by the fact that she was fascinated and could read all the London bus numbers by the age of three. She recently won an academic scholarship at Presbyterian Ladies' College in Perth, where she took up debating, taking after her papa. Her love of animals and nature mean that she loves all the time the family spend in Africa and she believes that one day she may live there.

Nisha has just participated in the global round of the World Scholar's Cup after qualifying as the sixth highest scoring team in the Perth round. The global round this year was held in Bangkok with over 3,400 students from over fifty countries. This is an academic competition which this year had the theme of an Imperfect World covering debating, writing and a rigorous exam in various World Scholar's Cup subjects including history, science, arts, social studies, special area and literature and the Scholar's Bowl with the team working together to solve thoughtful creative challenges related to the theme. Nisha's team came fifth in the Australia and Americas region and have qualified for Tournament of Champions to be held at Yale University later this year. Nisha was the top junior scholar of her school, won over ten medals at the event and won an award in the Overall Scholar's Competition. She is now off to London for a holiday where she is intending to compete in a couple of tennis tournaments. She has been playing a lot of tennis and has recently won a couple of tournaments in Perth as well as being the Under 18 Open Girls champion of the local tennis club when she was eleven. Nisha also continues to play viola, percussion and pipe drums and is a member of five music ensembles.

Born in 2006, Ross is a pupil at Scotch College in Perth. He shares Nisha's love of maths and is passionate about all sport, in particular, cricket and tennis. If he could play cricket and tennis all day he would be very happy. Ross enjoys chess club at school and likes putting what he has learned there into practice when he plays chess with his papa. Ross continues to play guitar and enjoys chess, Aussie Rules football, basketball and tennis. He has recently been elected as library captain.

Born in 2008, Natasha attends Presbyterian Ladies' College. A big character with a huge personality, she does well at school, but probably rather likes the social aspect of school above everything else. Natasha loves spending time with everyone at home creating art, writing stories or playing with her younger brother Marcus. She loves books and one of her favourite pastimes is reading books with her nana. Natasha is playing violin and and is very much enjoying netball and tennis. She is hoping to start playing in tournaments soon and is starting basketball this year.

Born in 2010, Marcus is a pupil at Scotch College. Quirky, charming and fun, he is also very caring, loving and affectionate. He swims well and plays tennis. He constantly disappears from home to visit his nana and papa, usually taking a book he wants read or a game he wants to play. He has a great zest for life and enthusiasm for everything. Marcus is enjoying being in first year at Scotch College. He has taken up violin and will soon join the orchestra. He enjoys playing chess, tennis, hockey and soccer.

Born in 1998, like her papa, Imogen excels at public speaking and debating. She was captain of the NSW schools' debating team and won the National Schools competition in Adelaide. As well as being awarded with the best speaker of the tournament prize, she was appointed as captain of the Australian team for the competition in Singapore in 2015, reaching the quarter-finals. She was the second best speaker in the tournament overall – who does she take after?! She is now debating for Sydney University. In late June 2015, she came to Perth for a debating competition and it was our pleasure to have her and her delightful boyfriend James to dinner. Imogen has turned out to be a beautiful and charming woman.

Born in 2002, Harriet also excels at debating. She loves animals, science and, recently qualified as a scuba diver, she loves diving at the Great Barrier Reef. She wants to be a marine biologist and nothing is likely to stand in her way if she wants to achieve that goal.

Born in 2006, Hamish loves chess and Minecraft. The official Cranbrook (primary school) tuba player, he wants to be an astronaut and is already studying hard to achieve this goal. He has the same love of arguing a position that is apparent in both of his sisters.

I am very fortunate to have such a splendid family. And I'm proud of each and every one of them.

29

REFLECTIONS

My father died at the age of sixty-four, my brother in his early seventies and my mother in her eighties. I must have my mother's genes – the Simpson genes. I turned eighty-one on 20th March 2016 and am still going strong. I cannot believe it and I certainly do not deserve it. I have a loving wife, three loving children and seven grandchildren. And all lovable. Perhaps I may become a great grandfather, who knows? When I think about it, to be in my eighties, in such a position with so many happy memories, I am indeed a most lucky lad.

What do you do in your eighties? Well, first of all, thank someone you are still alive and in good health. Keep busy. Play bridge and keep the brain active as well. Try to be a better husband. A better father and a better grandfather. And hope you will become a happy and contented great grandfather. I have a recipe for enjoying my life: keep the brain active and memories flowing.

What am I doing just now? Finishing a second (perhaps a third) glass of Oyster Bay wine, a coffee and a cigar, being commanded to play chess by my grandson, young Marcus, and watching cricket, tennis or football on TV. Is it a tough life here in Australia? Certainly not. But it's still interesting and stimulating. I am a lucky bounder.